com·mun·ion: /kəˈmyo͞onyən/ *noun:* the sharing or exchanging of intimate thoughts and feelings, especially when the exchange is on a mental or spiritual level.

COMMUNION

2020

AND THE MIDDLE PATH BACK TO REASON, MORALITY AND EACH OTHER

JEFF KRASNO

Published in The United States of America by Commune Media, Inc.

Book design by Alicia Greenleaf

ISBN 978-0-578-86135-7
e-Book ISBN 978-0-578-86134-0

Printed by Bookmark in Canada

www.onecommune.com

Dedicated to my father, Richard,
who gave me words.

Acknowledgements

My deep gratitude to:

Schuyler, my editor-in-life.
Jake, friend and partner, for putting the pencil in my hand.
My daughters, Phoebe, Lolli and Micah, for being (mostly) willing subjects.
Jean Krasno, for bequeathing me persistence and creativity.
Eric, Lauren and Lewis Krasno.
Ann Grant, my mother-in-law and #1 fan.
Christen Vidanovic, for sherpa'ing this book into reality.
Alicia Greenleaf, who made it beautiful.

The Commune team: Austin, Megan, Beau, Adra, Ramneet, Travis,
Luis, Kelly, Jodi, Jess, Ruby and Shayla.

My Commune partners for their belief in our vision: Brendon Burchard,
Jeffrey Walker, Briohny Smyth, Grant Harling, George Hagerman,
Andrew Creighton, Ian Lopatin, Jodi Blea, Dhru Purohit, David DeKadt,
Richard Krasno, Adriene Mishler, Jimmy Mulvihill, Chip Conley,
Carlos Garcia, Tom Windish, Paul Hawken, Craig Clemens, Amin Maredia,
Malcolm CasSelle, Gunnar Lovelace, Jake Capps, Charlie Hartwell, Bo Shao,
Patrick McKenna, Shelby Clark, Julius Mokrauer, Rachel Sheinbein,
Joe Greenstein, and Seth Tabatznik.

My podcast team: Sebastian & Ryan.

Sam Harris, Russell Brand, Charles Eisenstein, Brene Brown, Marianne
Williamson, Yuval Noah Harari, and (the late) Wayne Dyer for inspiration.

All of the brilliant Commune Teachers: Adriene Mishler,
Andrew Sealy, Anita Moorjani, Brendon Burchard, Briohny Smyth,
Byron Katie, Charles Eisenstein, Chelsey Korus, Colleen Saidman Yee,
Danielle LaPorte, Deepak Chopra, Dr. Chelsea Jackson Roberts,
Dr. Jolene Brighten, Dr. Mark Hyman, Dr. Mary Pardee,
Dr. Michael Breus, Dr. Pedram Shojai, Dr. Rebecca Branstetter,
Emi Guereca, Emily Schromm, Evelyn Carter, Finian Makepeace,
Jacqueline Suskin, Jacy Cunningham, Jason Wrobel, Jennifer Elliot,
Jennifer Partridge, Joy Reese, Julie Oliver, Justine Malick,
Kate Nelson, Kimberly Snyder, Lauren Handel Zander, Light Watkins,
Marianne Williamson, Mary Beth LaRue, Matt Phippen,
Michael B. Beckwith, Nick Ortner, Noah Mazé, Preethaji Krishna,
Rodney Yee, Rosie Acosta, Russell Brand, Schuyler Grant,
Scott Schwenk, Seane Corn, Sharon Salzberg, Sophia Amoruso,
Sophie Jaffe, Tommy Rosen, Tracee Stanley, and Wim Hof.

Additional thanks to Julia Dancyger, Anasa Troutman, Ara Katz,
Heather Story, Charlie Briggs, Sean Hoess, Karina MacKenzie,
and Kitty Cowles.

The Commune community: the thousands of messages you
have sent me, both supportive and critical, have fueled the work
and made me better.

2020 CHRONOLOGY

Introduction

Dear Reader,

In mid-March, as the human ship anchored into Port Lockdown, my dearest friend and colleague, Jacob, urged me to begin writing a weekly essay for our burgeoning Commune community. Naively, I agreed. And these toiled-over Sunday screeds took on the playful, if slightly irritating, rubric Commusing.

The cocktail of pandemic, quarantine and social media induced a global drunkenness of anxiety and fear. By leveraging words as vessels for emotions, I hoped I could help people make a modicum of sober sense out of this confounding and uncertain time.

Of course, when I penned the first missive in late March, I could not presage how tumultuous and indelible the year 2020 would be. Over time, these weekly exhortations dispatched to a million scattered souls across the globe became a sort of communion, a series of intimate spiritual conversations.

Through no premeditation, these articles took the form of biographical creative non-fiction, a genre of which I was completely unaware. Every week, I sharpened my pencil to lay my soul bare, swinging the door wide open into the madcap yarns of my family life with the hope that people might find their own stories within mine. Stories breed empathy, the donning of another's emotional clothing, and forge connection in an increasingly atomized and lonely world.

The topics for these essays were juiced right out of the lemon of 2020. I traversed the bristly socio-political landscape of COVID-19, racial justice, the psychological impacts of social media, the end of shared reality and, of course, the American election. Interspersed, I have explored the perennial spiritual riddles of fatherhood, grief, death and the emergence of new life.

Somewhere along the line, I innocently began to attach my personal email to these articles and on Sunday afternoon the deluge of weekly responses crested the bow of my inbox; notes that expressed gratitude and others that would break your heart in two. Oftentimes, I would send readers my phone number and just listen when they called. People, above all else, just want to be heard.

In an era of sensationalism and hyper politicization, I attempt to step out of the political invective, cultivate awareness of biases and find a middle way. And I implore you to do the same. In 2020, the world seemed all too often patently insane. In this compendium of collected essays, I attempt to bushwhack a pathway back to sanity through reason, secular morality and a smattering of dubious dad humor.

In many ways, these writings have been an exercise in my own personal development transpiring in public. Writing demands thought and through this, often arduous, process of reflection, I have grown. And, in this book, I invite you to do the same. Attached to the essays are writing exercises, evocations for contemplation that will lead you to a better understanding of the world and yourself. Writing is a great gift you can bequeath yourself, particularly when you are less preoccupied with the product and enveloped in the process. Unwittingly, you emerge from it wiser, if slightly malodorous.

This book is in many ways reflective of my broader work on Earth. It seeks to build a sturdy bridge that spans the islands of our personal and societal well-being, to help us see our own individual lives as part of a bigger human project, to foster a communion with a higher spirit and with each other.

Thanks for reading so far. It's an honor to do this work.

In love, include me,

Jeff

GO TO YOUR ROOM

APRIL 5

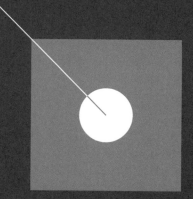

In December of 2019, the first outbreak of a novel coronavirus was detected in Wuhan, China. The virus spread from China to Europe, and inevitably to America. In late January of 2020, the first US covid-19 patient was identified in Washington State.

By March 11, 2020, the World Health Organization declared it a global pandemic. It was the first true pandemic since the Spanish Flu of 1918. Many states began to combat the disease with shelter-in-place orders. As panic spread in the early spring, grocery stores ran out of supplies, including toilet paper and cleaning supplies.

By early April, 9,400 people were recorded dead from COVID-19, although the true death toll was likely higher. Almost 7 million people had filed for unemployment due to economic contraction stemming from the lockdown measures. Overstretched Emergency Rooms and healthcare workers had limited supplies to deal with a growing viral pandemic with still unknown effects. Across the country, many had older family members dying alone in the hospital, with no way to say goodbye to their loved ones. The first quarantine was only just beginning. Finding connection through apps like Zoom, and activities like baking sourdough bread, were common escapes from the pervading sense of aloneness.

I adore my younger brother, Eric. I was his keeper for thirteen fraught years, managing his exceptional musical talents. There are many clichés that warn against mixing business with family but we not only speak to each other, we actually seek out each other's company. We litigated all of our disputes in elementary school.

When Eric and I were five and ten respectively, our dad purchased one of the world's first VHS players. This feat of engineering was a proper piece of furniture, mahogany-paneled and so weighty a grown man could barely lift it. When the system arrived, it came with four video cassettes: the original *Grease, Star Wars, The Empire Strikes Back* and a naughty masterwork named *Inside Desiree Cousteau*. My brother and I so coveted the latter that its name still lives on my tongue. My father disappeared this treasure early on and, candidly, Eric and I passed the better part of our youth rummaging through the attic and under my dad's bed in search of it. We found other things of significant interest, but never Ms. Cousteau.

In her absence, we settled for the Star Wars films. The videotapes we had acquired were most certainly not officially distributed by Mr. Lucas. They were bootlegs shot by some two-bit hustler in the back of a theater. Despite the shakiness of the camera work, I became obsessed with this intergalactic battle between light and dark. I so cherished these films that I kept the tapes in a purple felt Courvoisier bag that I nicked from the family bar.

I could recite the lines of these epics better than Spielberg himself. Every Halloween, I donned my Jedi cape, seized my lightsaber and skywalked across Tatooine bringing home a Death Star's supply of peanut butter cups. For Christmas and my birthday, Star Wars merchandise filled the wish list from top to bottom. I collected all the figurines: Luke, Han, Leia, Lando, Obi Wan, Chewy, R2. We were on a first name basis. I housed them all in a giant Darth Vader briefcase that featured little cubbies for each of them.

My brother knew how much I treasured these miniature collectibles and he made it his hobby to furtively purloin them on the regular. He hid them among his worthless hodgepodge of baubles in a large green

Most of us are simply not trained to deal with our minds in isolation. Blaise Pascal famously wrote, "All of humanity's problems stem from man's inability to sit quietly in a room alone."

plastic frog. When I noticed one missing, I would stormtroop down the hallway, hurtle through the door and plunge into the frog. I considered it a rebel mission but, inevitably, it was a trap. For as soon as I was in his room, Eric would scream for mom or dad and levy false claims of physical abuse. This accusation evoked the wrath of my beleaguered parents who doled out the ultimate punishment: "Go to your room, Jeffrey, and don't come out until dinner."

My protestations were futile. I would mope into my room and flop on to the bed vowing never to speak to my brother again. That, of course, barely lasted an hour.

The most severe punishment that can be dispensed to a child, besides the corporal, is imposed solitude. Isolation is psychologically traumatizing to human beings of every age. Merely the idea of sequestration can be stressful. Ten minutes before my parent's reprimand, I might be amusing myself happily in my room – alone without feeling lonely – but exiled against my will I would wallow in the meaninglessness of life.

As a species wired for connection, aloneness can be torturous. And this torment follows us into adulthood in myriad cultural manifestations, large and small. When ejected from the game, a basketball player is prohibited from lingering on the end of the bench. Instead, he is relegated to the locker room to contemplate his misdeeds alone. In the judicial system, the most severe form of punishment short of the death penalty is solitary confinement.

Most of us are simply not trained to deal with our minds in isolation. Blaise Pascal famously wrote, "All of humanity's problems stem from man's inability to sit quietly in a room alone."

Yet, suddenly, psychological quarantine is where many of us find ourselves; sheltering-in-place, divorced from our communal routines.

The pandemic has conjured a moment of extreme mobilization for healthcare professionals, food providers, grocery clerks, delivery drivers, scientists, and government workers. The stress endured by these brave, essential souls will be severe. The rest of us, however, are being called, asymmetrically, to inaction.

We've been sent to our respective rooms. And, ironically, the most noble thing we can do for one another is distance from each other. This helps our essential superheroes by flattening the curve, but, in this inaction, we are left alone with our minds.

In isolation and uncertainty, the untrained mind often defaults to fear. One begins to identify with the emotion which only reinforces the ego, the false notion of the separate self. The ability to think critically erodes and one becomes susceptible to outlandish theories. The monkey mind flourishes, swinging recklessly from branch to branch, compounding chaos. One seeks satisfaction and solace through external stimuli – whiskey, weed, Facebook likes, nutter butters, Amazon – pick your poison.

Like a dancer trains her legs for a jete, so must we train our minds. It may seem like a meditation practice is effete and dispensable during a bloody global pandemic. Nurses are intubating and the ill are struggling to breathe – while little old me needs to go "sit" on a paisley pillow and witness my breath to avoid a panic attack. But let me upend any notion that this practice is superfluous. For those battling the front lines of this scourge, even thirty seconds of Vipassana can relieve stress. If there's any group that needs to remain in their pre-frontal cortex, it's doctors and emergency room workers.

This practice is no less important for those of us sequestered in our internet caves. In the absence of IRL communication, our attention has become a sought-after commodity. We are fending off a meteor shower of information – some of it sound, some of it faulty. Social media is slinging poisoned arrows at us from every angle. How can we see the road ahead when 24-hour news cycle is fogging up the windshield of truth?

We need to cultivate a peace of mind that neuters fear and fosters discernment. We must hone the ability to peel away fallacy from fact. Meditation helps us disassociate from our emotions, witness them and not be them. It provides us with the power of equanimity. It boosts the immune systems, improves sleep and fortifies healthy habits. It gives us the presence, off the cushion, to notice if we're touching our face or remembering to wash our hands.

While no one would choose a cramped, armored cell as their primary residence, solitude need not always be a banishment. It is often an opportunity to grow, to cultivate wisdom. Why do monks choose the monastery? Why do people seek spiritual retreat in an ashram? Or more relevant to this missive, why did Yoda find refuge in Dagobah, a remote world of swamps and forests?

In the hush of seclusion, we may discover a plane of consciousness unbound by space, time, location and form. Our busy, noisy quotidian lives are circumscribed by our five senses. We hear across a finite frequency range from 20 Hz to 20 kHz. We see within a spectrum between infra-red to ultra-violet. We taste across five flavor profiles. These limitations define our subjective special reality. But what lies beyond?

Yoda called it "the Force." Of course, we remember the splashier bits of it like telekinesis, the ability to move and manipulate objects with one's mind. Though I spent entire afternoons staring intently at my lava lamp trying to move it across the night stand, I never did succeed in defying the laws of physics. But, in retrospect, this undistracted focus may have been my first meditation session.

The force has other cosmic aspects including telepathy and enhanced metaphysical perception. But these super powers are not the qualities that make Yoda so venerable. (I mean, wouldn't we all would choose to be Yoda? Despite his utter homeliness.)

It's a stretch, but close your eyes for a moment and envision Yoda at the grocery store. He's filled his basket, most likely with green leafy vegetables, and is ready to check out. He approaches the register and, alas, there is a short queue. It will take no more than five minutes before Yoda will meticulously arrange his vegan delights on the the conveyor belt. Does Yoda instinctively pull out his phone to assuage the momentary boredom? Of course not. He stands in line, patient and tranquil, and processes an idea or simply observes the goings-on. He lends a hand, perhaps magically slipping just the right coupon to a stranger in need.

In the hush of seclusion, we may discover a plane of consciousness unbound by space, time, location and form. Our busy, noisy quotidian lives are circumscribed by our five senses. We hear across a finite frequency range from 20 Hz to 20 kHz. We see within a spectrum between infra-red to ultra-violet. We taste across five flavor profiles. These limitations define our subjective special reality. But what lies beyond?

Yoda's mind is not distracted. His thoughts are not fragmented. He single-tasks. We revere Yoda because he embodies the qualities of a sage: patience, discernment, benevolence, serenity, timeliness, focus and wisdom.

This way of living is available to you, even in this madness, perhaps especially in the solitude of this strange time. You may not ever move a tie-fighter out of a bog with your mind but you might be able to not look at your phone at a traffic light. Or be present with your children. Or read a book. Or maybe even write one.

You don't need the Millennium Falcon to cultivate this life, though using Yoda's mystical sentence construction of object-subject-verb can be helpful. To distant galaxies one need travel not. On an inward journey a Jedi Grand Master must go.

Right here, in this forced monasticism, "You must unlearn what you have learned. Try not. Do, or do not. There is no try."

Throughout this book there will be writing exercises based upon the themes of the preceding essay. Prior to engaging with these prompts, I encourage everyone to take a moment to reflect or meditate with the purpose of bringing clarity to your work. Below you will find a very simple meditation that you may employ throughout this book and in your life generally.

MEDITATION

Find a quiet place to sit, either on the ground with your legs crossed and your back straight, or in a chair, with both feet on the ground and your hands on your thighs. Close your eyes. Slowly count to four as you take a deep breath in, and then pause, holding your breath at the top of your inhale. Gently release your exhale as you slowly count to six in your mind. Repeat this exercise 3 times and then let your breath return to normal, as you sit with your eyes closed, just breathing.

As thoughts come into your mind, gently acknowledge them and let them pass, like clouds floating by in the sky. Try to sit in this space for a few minutes. If you'd like, set a timer for 5 minutes so that you aren't worried about checking how much time has passed.

When you feel lost in your thoughts, just return your attention to your breath.

WRITING EXERCISES

How do you feel when you are alone?

_____

_____

_____

_____

_____

_____

What thoughts and emotions come up for you when you are alone?

_____

_____

_____

_____

_____

_____

Are you able to witness yourself attaching to a particular feeling or thought?

_____

_____

_____

_____

_____

What happens when your mind jumps from thought to thought?

_____

_____

_____

_____

Try to recall a positive memory of being alone and write about it.

_____

_____

_____

_____

_____

_____

_____

_____

_____

_____

_____

_____

_____

_____

MAYBE
APRIL 12

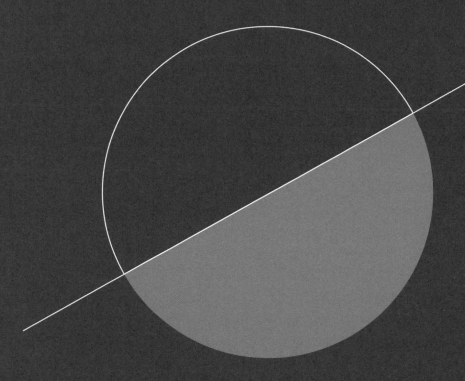

While the pope delivered his Easter message from a closed St. Peter's Basilica and organists played to empty cathedrals for livestreamed vigils, many sought to create sacred spaces in their own backyards— discovering the holy sounds of spring songbirds and contemplating the universal suffering that swept the globe. Church leaders grappled with how to provide a sense of spiritual connection while abiding by the need for social distancing. Some contracted the virus, and paid the ultimate price, after defying the state's guidance to close down places of worship. The contrast of the need for spiritual community and the need to protect our vulnerable was sharp, bringing into greater focus deeper questions about how we approach the spiritual in our lives.

Growing up in the Northeast, I looked forward to springtime with the same giddy, restless anticipation that inflected the rollout of each new Star Wars installment.

The air, at long last, humid and warm against my face, infused with the perfume of thawed earth, tasted of sweet possibility.

No longer bound in my winter gear, I'd sidle down to the bus stop in my Stan Smith's and my short-sleeved Izod. Bees went back to business and basketball courts buzzed again. We'd play late into the stretching daylight and come home awful dirty and good tired.

Around the house, the ritual of outdoor chores was resurrected. We peeled off the pool cover and shocked the murky water. We took down the storm windows and put up the screens. We dug out the garden beds and neatly trenched new rows.

By the time I was 10, I had usurped the lawn-mowing duties from my dad. Every April, I would exhume the apple red lawn tractor from the bowels of the garage, wipe it down, pump the tires, check the belts, adjust the blade levels and gas it up. Grumpy Old Red preferred his winter hibernation and needed significant cajoling to turn over. Eventually, he complied. Every Saturday morning, I mounted him like an old steed and set off mowing. Halfway through the expansive back yard, the olfactory elixir of cut grass, midday sun and diesel fuel drugged me into a hazy horticultural trance.

There are always a few chores that kids outwardly bemoan but secretly enjoy. Mowing the lawn evoked an odd sort of subdued optimism in me. Maybe because no matter how fine a job I did, by the next Saturday, the grass, proudly grown back, would be pertly awaiting my ministrations. This groundskeeping stint was my first visceral experience with nature's unflinching ability to renew itself. The deciduous elm or maple sheds and regenerates its foliage. A polluted river can recover on its own. As evidenced by the clearing skies over Beijing and crystalline canals of Venice, nature thrives when we leave it alone.

Springtime is back again, thumbing its nose at winter and shading its eyes from Summer's inevitability. The tilting of the earth on its axis toward the sun pays little mind to the coronavirus. But, of course, we do. The optimism of vernal rejuvenation is clouded by uncertainty. Though we're not kind to her, Mother Earth commonly shrugs her shoulders. This year however, have we pushed her too far? Nature cycles forward unabated, but the rhythms of humanity have been stunted and twisted. Either nature is having a reckoning with us or we are having one with ourselves. Perhaps there is little difference. We are now being pressed to examine what we have long taken for granted, to question the bedrock of the human story.

April's budding trees are reflected in ancient human tales of renascence. The Pagan *Ostara*, or Spring Equinox, marks the day when light and darkness are once again in balance, with light on the rise. Last week, Jews observed Passover, celebrating the delivery of the Israelites out of Egyptian slavery. This Sunday, Christians celebrate Easter, which commemorates the Resurrection of Jesus on the third day after his Crucifixion.

These holy days are a reminder that the human story has long been one of suffering and redemption, death and rebirth. Through the wound comes the salve.

While wisdom may sit behind pain, it is rarely visible in the midst of it. Humanity is now enduring great hardship. People are falling ill and struggling to breathe. Doctors, nurses, supply chain workers, delivery people and grocery clerks are battling on the front lines. Unemployment is soaring and millions are struggling to make ends meet. In a season typically marked by open doors and blithe freedom, we are locked down, grappling with fear, anxiety and loneliness.

But this moment of privation also holds the promise of possibility. Society's addictions – from fossil fuels to junk food, from rampant consumerism to unchecked busy-ness – has put us on a perilous trajectory. But, this spring, our patterns of behavior are shifting by necessity. Fast food has slowed down and our ovens are firing. Our cars are idle, but our legs are moving. Our airports lie fallow while our neighborhoods are stirring. Lurking in the shadows of the uncertainty and chaos, there is a seed germinating, begging us to ask more of ourselves and each other. In the dark soul of the night, a voice whispers:

Maybe cooking is better than going out?

Maybe less convenience is more fulfilling?

Maybe remote work is more efficient and better for the environment?

Maybe I don't need so many new clothes and devices?

Maybe I actually like my kids, and, more surprisingly, maybe they even like me?

Maybe growing a carrot makes it taste better?

Maybe I should know my neighbors' name?

Maybe I don't need to travel the world?

Maybe God is exactly where I am?

Maybe if enough people embrace a simpler way of life
then we can define new metrics of collective success?

Maybe the myth of the need for endless growth can wither away?

Maybe we can create sustainable local economies that don't require
exploitation of anonymous workers and landscapes around the globe?

Maybe we can rediscover a passion for civic engagement and reinvigorate the public square?

Maybe there is a new human story being birthed?

Maybe.

WRITING EXERCISES

The coronavirus pandemic impacted everyone on the planet.
Think back on the year 2020 and write about some of your most potent memories.

What did you discover about yourself that surprised you?

4.12

Did any of your priorities change over the year? If so, write about this transformation.

Did you develop any new routines due to the quarantines?

How has your life changed for the better or worse during this strange time?

WE ARE ENOUGH

APRIL 19

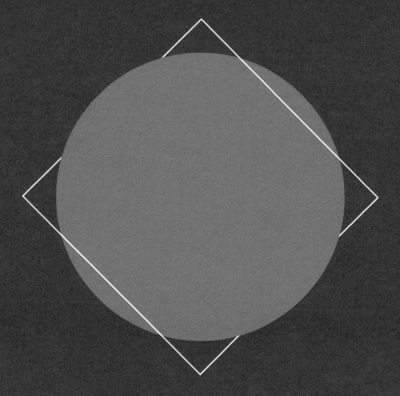

As the world crested the first spike in coronavirus transmission, there was immense pressure to re-open the economy. When an initial small business loan program quickly ran dry, an additional 450-billion-dollar relief package was finally agreed upon. The package funded the Paycheck Protection Program, the SBA's disaster relief fund and provided billions more for hospitals and testing, but the process was filled with glitches and frustration for small business owners and much of the funding went to large corporations. Outbreaks spread quickly through nursing homes, claiming 7,000 lives, a fifth of COVID-19 related deaths in the U.S. at the time. Retail and restaurant spending suffered its sharpest drop in almost 30 years, as business owners struggled to stay afloat. Unemployment rates rose to 23 million, the highest in the data's history.

Soon enough, you will feel the gale force winds of corporate globalism chafing your face. It will scream, "Back to normal!" — a clarion call to return to the shopping mall, book that vacation trip, buy that new television. These messages will be cloaked in patriotic slogans like "support American workers."

The refrain of unbridled global capitalism will once again trumpet images of unattainable success and perfection in an attempt to convince you that you are not enough. And then market you trinkets and services to address your perceived deficiencies.

If only, and only if, you buy this designer dress... will you be beautiful.

Of course, the rush of excitement fades almost as soon as you open the box. But also consider the journey of that dress; from the cotton fields of Arkansas to the yarn-making factories of Indonesia; the cloth was made, cut and dyed in Bangladesh and sewn in a Chinese sweatshop, shipped to a distribution center in Bakersfield, trucked to an H&M in Anaheim; and finally ... to you.

Now that we have felt the looming shadow of the grim reaper, Armageddon's hot breath on our necks. Now that we've hunkered down with our families: cooking, reading, praying, walking, crying, laughing... holding each other tighter than before, sometimes from six feet away. Now that we have awakened to what makes life sacred and worthwhile, we know this:

We are enough. Right here in our pajamas. We are enough.

We can envision a new human story, once obscured by smog, but now visible on the horizon, not solely because we've awakened, but because we stopped spewing filth into our skies.

Now we can see that not only does endless consumption fail to serve us but it also does not serve the worker, American or foreign. It contributes to a society where three people own more wealth than 50% of

We have imagined a world in which we own less things, lest we be owned by our things.

the population combined, to a country that has left our most vulnerable citizens destitute on the streets, to a system that has under-equipped our brave health care workers.

In our quarantine, something shifted. Quietly, as if out of a collective unconscious, we imagined the same thing:

We have imagined a local, community-based approach to living with systems and structures engineered at human-scale, not at global industrial scale.

We have imagined new indices of success measured by how we treat our most vulnerable citizens and our planet.

We have imagined a new enlightenment that alloys science with the universal spiritual principles echoed across all traditions: love, compassion, empathy and tolerance.

We have imagined a world in which we own less things, lest we be owned by our things.

This is my humble prayer: As we are beckoned back to "normal" let us not be tempted by the siren call of consumption. Let us remember that bending the arc of history can start in your backyard with a garden and by bringing soup to a sick neighbor.

Let us remember the things that, in our shelter, made life worthwhile.

Let us remember that we are enough.

WRITING EXERCISES

The coronavirus pandemic was a catalyst for a slew of lifestyle changes, especially in the early days. Think about how your relationship to your previous lifestyle changed, and how it impacted your perspective of what really mattered.

What are the components of life that make living most worthwhile?

_____

_____

_____

_____

_____

_____

How did COVID-19 make you more aware of these essential elements of life?

_____

_____

_____

_____

_____

Do you seek happiness through the acquisition of material objects?
What "things" could you do without?

_____

_____

_____

_____

_____

Do you live a locally-focused life? In what ways do you think a more local existence
could yield a happier and healthier planet?

_____

_____

_____

_____

_____

THE NEW FRONTIER
APRIL 22

April 22, 2020 was the 50th anniversary of Earth Day, which began as a national and bipartisan conservation movement marked by protests and rallies that took place across the entire country.

In 1960, President Kennedy captivated our collective imagination with The New Frontier. This bold vision proposed the unfathomable notion of putting a man on the moon.

It took nine years, but when Apollo 11 transmitted those first images taken from space, it forever changed our relationship to the planet we call home. Surely you have seen them; a beautiful, delicate singular orb, luminescent green-blue without the imaginary lines of nationhood; one world unfractured by distinctions of race, religion, ethnicity, or sexual orientation.

It is no wonder that, in 1970, less than a year after the Giant Leap, we celebrated the first Earth Day, established the EPA, made major amendments to the Clean Air Act and, two years later, passed the Clean Water Act.

We were galvanized into action by a vision bigger than ourselves. Our consciousness shifted. A critical mass of individuals worldwide imagined a better version of ourselves as stewards of a shared planet. But this proved to be a fragile revolution.

Fifty years after the first Earth Day, we find ourselves in a wicked paradox. While humans have fallen ill, Mother Nature has shown signs of emergent well-being.

The skies have cleared. For the first time in decades, the Himalayas have become visible on the Indian horizon. Since Italy went into lockdown, NO2 levels in Milan have fallen by about 40 percent. Los Angeles has seen a 30 percent decrease in PM2.5, a form of pollution composed of particles smaller than a strand of human hair that can cause lung disease and heart ailments. Earth Systems Professor Marshall Burke estimates that the decrease in PM2.5 likely saved 77,000 lives in China alone.

The Venice canals are resplendently aglow, sheep crowd the crosswalks of Scotland, and traffic levels in Britain are equivalent to 1955. The price of oil crashed because there is no place to store the surplus. We're not using it.

If we grapple with these sacrifices now, small and large, individual and collective, can we avert the looming cataclysms of environmental breakdown? No matter how challenging this moment, this suffering cowers in the impending menace of drought and starvation, fire and flood, mass migration and war that an overexploited planet promises.

Certainly, a global pandemic is not a long-term moral solution to our planetary dis-ease. The loss of human life is not an environmental strategy.

How do we leverage this inflection point for our collective benefit, to re-envision a sustainable tenancy on this planet while also honoring the disparity of human experiences in this moment?

Many are sick, some are dying. Some are on the front lines. Many have lost work. And others are hunkered down, in a coerced monasticism, vacillating between anxiety and the epiphany that less may be more. Of those who have paid the ultimate price, the data are showing they are disproportionately the most vulnerable among us, toiling in essential jobs that cannot be done on Zoom.

My instinct tells me that, in order to right ourselves, the world will need to withstand a lot of pain. And that pain will not be evenly distributed when Nature collects its debt.

But is there a degree of "suffering" we must endure to ensure the health of the planet and our viability on it?

Can the world withstand hundreds of millions unemployed in service of right-sizing the Chinese coal industry, factory farming, Exxon-Mobil, Aramco, Coca-Cola, Nestle, McDonald's and others that engage in unsustainable practices?

Can we sacrifice the convenience of fast food, overnight shipping, whimsical travel and pre-packaged everything?

Can we find the will to upturn the systems and structures that have desecrated the earth in the name of commercial profits?

Can we honor those who have passed away by instantiating a new world story that breaks our narrative of separation from nature?

Can we apply metrics of growth to human happiness rather than corporate top-lines?

If we grapple with these sacrifices now, small and large, individual and collective, can we avert the looming cataclysms of environmental breakdown? No matter how challenging this moment, this suffering cowers in the impending menace of drought and starvation, fire and flood, mass migration and war that an overexploited planet promises.

We stand today on the edge of a New Frontier. However, we seek not the stars, but an inner reckoning.

We must now do the soulful work of determining our true needs and sources of fulfillment; to revise everything from our global economy to our daily pleasures. And to manifest this discovery with profound acts of conscience, creativity, and sacrifice in service of humanity and our planet.

On this 50th Earth Day, we bend this refrain for our New Frontier:

"Ask not what your planet can do for you, ask what you can do for your planet."

WRITING EXERCISES

The coronavirus pandemic inspired many of us with clear skies and a simpler lifestyle, while simultaneously increasing our reliance on take-out and packaging.

How did you see your environmental footprint change during the 2020/2021 coronavirus pandemic? What positive things changed? What was more difficult?

_____

_____

_____

_____

_____

_____

_____

_____

_____

_____

_____

What sacrifices are you willing to make in order to create a healthier world? Which ones seem overwhelming or unattainable?

_____

_____

_____

_____

_____

_____

_____

_____

_____

_____

Describe the place you live in its most beautiful and healthy state. Who is there? What does it look like? Are there plants or animals? Imagine a new story for your home, or the planet, and include yourself in it.

GIANT STEPS

MAY 3

I have been learning Giant Steps on the piano. Penned by the legendary saxophonist John Coltrane in 1959, it was a revolutionary piece of music that upended the traditional harmony of be-bop jazz. It became a litmus test among players, distinguishing the neophytes from those capable of fusing virtuosic chops and emotional magnificence. But it wasn't Coltrane's technical prowess that bent the arc of music.

Coltrane challenged the status quo with a deep expression of the heart — profound wailings from the spiritual well, built atop the technical well. We heard him not with our ears, we heard him with our soul.

Yet here I am, plodding through it as if I am taking a multiple-choice driver's test, just praying I can get to the end with enough right answers, and my mind wanders to this: What are the components of great art? And, perhaps by extension, a great society?

Certainly, it's not just technical ability. Great music is not a stream of perfectly executed scales. Portraiture is not meant to mirror photography. Soaring oratory is not a recitation of facts (though I'll gladly take some facts right now).

In art, we thirst to unshackle ourselves from the ordered ordinary, to wander into the limbic. No matter how well-sanded any prose might be, if it doesn't give me a splinter, if I don't cry or laugh when writing it, if my heart does not leap in some fashion, then it is bound for the dustbin.

Epiphanous art alloys technique and expression, empiricism and revelation, head and heart. And when transcendent creation springs forth, there is a remarkable effect: We all feel the same.

This is how the club, theatre, or gallery becomes a church. We walk in atomized, individuals among separate individuals, until we are enveloped by the voluptuous heart; a musical crescendo, or a piercingly authentic monologue, and suddenly everyone is wearing the same rapt expression.

In a way, we become the music, as notions of time, space, location and form – the elements that so often define our individual human experience – dissolve. The curtain pulls back on the illusory nature of self.

This synchrony of humanity cannot be simply explained through neuroscience. Why have we evolved to both create and experience transcendence through art, so that viewing a beautiful piece of art gives us the same feeling as being in love. We may all be simultaneously emitting dopamine. But the real question is why? What is this mystical force that animates the collective unconscious?

And as the reflection of our collective art, is culture any different? If our human experience walks the tightrope of the material and immaterial, then so must culture.

Increasingly, though, we dwell solely in the material world; one that defines us by our possessions and job titles, one in which we interact as transactional units, one that feels like my elementary school music teacher's metronomic rendition of Giant Steps, always regurgitated at 3 minutes, 40 seconds long.

The Enlightenment ushered in reason, rationality, and the scientific method. And we built the systems and structures of modernity around these principles, often for damn good reason.

Liberal democracy, in theory, tabulates the will of the people, a marked improvement from the divine right of kings. Capitalism maintains social stability through a (supposed) mutually beneficial economic relationship between people, and it has lifted throngs out of serfdom.

Science and reason have built the piping of society, the road and bridges, the factories and skyscrapers, the infrastructure that girds our busy lives. Technology has provided us with medical advancements that save lives and alleviate pain, agricultural technology that could feed all the citizens of the world, an Internet that democratizes access to education and information.

However, inherent to science and its method is value neutrality. We increasingly live in structures and systems that have become inhumane, devoid of the ethics of the heart. The result is too often medical innovation gets channeled towards the pharmaceutical industry,

Now is the time to set down the armaments of our reasoned positions, remove our armor, and speak and listen to each other from the heart.

agricultural advancement is sponsored by Monsanto, and the Internet is leveraged to spread misinformation and commodify our habits.

For America, or anywhere, to be great again, we must once again find our hearts.

We are collectively craving epiphany, often historically manifested by the uniting of inspiration and action: Moses parting the sea to lead the Israelites out of slavery; Martin Luther King marching across the bridge in Selma (an act often called praying with his feet); Julia Butterfly Hill living in a 180-foot-tall tree for 738 days to protest old-growth clear-cutting.

If great art merges the mechanical and mystical, then should not our society also value them in equal measure?

Are we not aching for brave leadership centered in the heart?

Are we not thirsting to once again all feel the same?

This is the moment to discard our petty political labels and let the heart usher us into the church of our common humanity.

Now is the time to set down the armaments of our reasoned positions, remove our armor, and speak and listen to each other from the heart.

The spiritual heart holds the sacred truths echoed by every prophet – love, compassion and empathy – and thus the heart should set the coordinates of our systems and structures.

This is the Giant Step the world now beckons us to take: Like John Coltrane, we must challenge the status quo with a Revolution of the Heart.

WRITING EXERCISES

Life is a balance between head and heart, reason and inspiration, empiricism and emotion, planning and whimsy.

Are you, in general, more led by your head or your heart?

_____

_____

In which parts of your life do you leverage reason over emotion?
How does this make you feel?

_____

_____

_____

_____

_____

_____

In which parts of your life are you more guided by inspiration?
How does this make you feel?

_____

_____

_____

_____

_____

_____

_____

_____

Do you remember a time when your heart led you to do something? What was the outcome?

_____

_____

_____

_____

_____

_____

_____

_____

_____

_____

_____

How, in your own life, can you make your brain and heart work in concert?

_____

_____

_____

_____

_____

_____

_____

_____

_____

_____

_____

_____

_____

_____

WOMEN LEADERS AND COVID-19

MAY 10

Throughout the world, women leaders of different countries have shown a firm, compassionate and effective strategy against the coronavirus pandemic. In March 2020, Jacinda Ardern, the liberal prime minister of New Zealand, joined forces with the conservative prime minister of Australia, to send bipartisan messaging about the significant restrictions on their countries. By early May, New Zealand had fewer than 100 active cases. In Germany, led by Angela Merkel, there was a significantly lower death count than in many other European countries. Other women-led countries like Taiwan and Finland, saw similar success.

Last week, my wife-for-life, Schuyler, commemorated 50 orbits around the sun.

From the imposed monasticism of quarantine, I etched her a clumsy love letter, alternately irreverent and doting. Having been yoked for 32 years, Schuyler and I have lost our taste for sanctimony and revel in verbal jousting. I share an excerpt with you here:

I sought in you an absurd collection of archetypes;
Nurturing mother offering her soft breast
And lithe nymphet capable of whimsical handstands.
Resilient feminist bread-winner and occasional wanton Jezebel

Despite the lack of script,
your thespian pedigree has served you (and me) well.
You have played each character with aplomb and warrant
nominations for numerous supporting roles.
The world anxiously awaits your next casting: nurse.

I sit here, sheltering-in-place on Mother's Day, watching her pirouette from task to task; wrangling our three daughters, keeping businesses afloat, sparring with Zoom to stream her next class.

And I am enveloped by a profound sense of awe and gratitude, not just for her, but for all mothers who walk the razor's edge of both baking and earning the bread, nursing both child and parent.

I envision, somewhat ridiculously, Schuyler as Durga the Hindu goddess, with a dozen arms, bearing not the weapons of ancient India but the tools of modernity: battered iPhone, corporate prospectus, digital thermometer, cast-iron pan, reusable diaper, kitty litter box, father's bedpan, and wheelbarrow of mulch.

Mothers manage not just to tame chaos but conduct it into symphonies, transforming dots of disparate color into a Little Girl in a Blue Armchair.

Where patriarchy has attempted to standardize every component of life

Mother Nature, too, finds its symbiosis in the vast biodiversity of distinct plants and animals, each of whom she casts to play a small role in the glorious theatre of life.

in the name of growth and operational efficiency, the mother perceives a sustainable beauty in the interconnected web of variety.

In this way, mothers are the holders of the sacred. They recognize the value in the unique and interrelated; the hand-sewn dress, the heirloom necklace, the local yoga studio, the garden-grown cock-eyed carrot.

Mother Nature, too, finds its symbiosis in the vast biodiversity of distinct plants and animals, each of whom she casts to play a small role in the glorious theatre of life.

For mothers, there is no single right answer or one single way to determine it. There is no false pride. There is nuance. There is "yes and..."

During COVID-19, we have witnessed our global female leaders foster social cohesion through a delicate balance of decisiveness and empathy. Without either chest thumping or sanctimony, female heads-of-state have produced superlative results through distributed leadership and emotional intelligence.

Norway's Prime Minister Erna Solberg deferred medical decisions to the scientists and took the unusual step of directly addressing the country's children, telling them in two press conferences that it was "permitted to be a little bit scared."

Armed with a doctorate in quantum chemistry, Germany's Angela Merkel kept her country's fatality toll under 5,000 through calm, clear public exposition and an unparalleled marshaling of the health care system.

Jacinda Ardern, New Zealand's premier, went hard on early quarantining, while also delivering empathetic "stay home, save lives" videos from her couch. She embraced a kindness-first approach urging New

Zealanders to look after their neighbors, take care of the vulnerable, and make sacrifices for the greater good.

Notably, Ardern gave birth to her first child last year in Auckland's public hospital while serving as Prime Minister, becoming the first world leader to take maternity leave while in office. As of now, only 18 people have died of COVID-19 in New Zealand.

Women make great leaders for the same reason they make great parents; they flourish in the grey zone between question and answer, mystery and manifestation. And this is what makes our mothers – the great ones, the difficult ones, the complicated ones, the devoted ones – endlessly fascinating to us.

Our entire life is a journey back to our mothers, back to the peaceful belonging of the womb, back to the oneness; a rematriation with the divine, the reunion of Jesus and Mary. As T.S. Eliot wrote, "to arrive where we started and know the place for the first time."

We pause today to honor all mothers, including our Mother Earth. And to pray this fraught time can serve as a modern Annunciation, that a new savior will be born within the divine mother of each of us, one that inspires us to craft beauty from chaos.

Take a moment to reflect on motherhood generally. Meditate on the extensive responsibilities a mother takes on as a means to appreciate their titanic importance in life.

Sketch out some of the earliest memories that you have of your mother.
Use all of your physical senses. Describe the emotions that you feel when thinking about her.

_____
_____
_____
_____
_____

Recount a story about your own mother.
Which of her traits are most prevalent in this story?

_____
_____
_____
_____
_____
_____

Describe how you see your mother reflected in you.

_____
_____
_____
_____
_____
_____
_____
_____

What were/are the qualities of your mother that you love/loved?
That you hate/hated?

_____

_____

_____

_____

_____

Do you carry any of these qualities into your own life? Which ones?

_____

_____

_____

_____

What are the character traits that make a good mother?

_____

_____

_____

_____

_____

How are those character traits also reflected in superlative leadership?

_____

_____

_____

_____

_____

_____

_____

ON DEATH

MAY 17

In January 2002, literally out of the ashes of 9/11, Schuyler opened Kula Yoga Project just blocks north of the World Trade Center. This humble little studio up four flights of crooked lime green stairs became home for the bereaved denizens of lower Manhattan. My office, on the second floor, gave me a front row seat to witness the power of yoga and community to heal.

It bent the arc of my life. It led me to found Wanderlust and 13 years later move to Los Angeles and build Wanderlust Hollywood, an admittedly less humble center for yoga culture. I emptied my soul into building this place. Like a bedraggled chimney sweep from a Dickens novel, I heaved myself out of the drywall soot every night with the vision of someday hosting the likes of Marianne Williamson, Deepak Chopra, Russell Brand, Wim Hof, Byron Katie and the other brilliant poets and mystics that gave my life meaning. It all happened.

In this very strange time, in the very same week, both Kula Tribeca and Wanderlust Hollywood closed their doors for good.

The meditator in me can appreciate that we are just experiencing transitory phenomena from moment to moment. But if I am the sky and emotions are just clouds, then I am shrouded in a fog of sorrow. I cannot pretend that these gathering places did not hold the sacred.

These passings are, of course, just small totems of a deeper global heartache.

The harsh awareness of our own mortality has never been more acute. The global pandemic, replete with its archetypes and memes, has shone a blinding light on our impermanence — the Grim reaper clutching a scythe collecting souls on a Miami beach, images of desolate post-apocalyptic urban streets.

Part of being human is the awareness of inevitable death. Homo sapiens roaming the Serengeti 100,000 years ago knew they were going to die, just like you and I know.

However, our conception of death has evolved significantly over the past few hundred years. Throughout the Middle Ages, death was inextricably fastened to religion. There was a sense of helpless resignation around our own mortality, as God served as playwright of life's final act.

When the Black Death emerged in the mid-14th century, it wasn't traced by epidemiologists to a market in Wuhan. (Though, ironically, scientists now believe it came along the Silk Road from East Asia.)

The plague, which killed almost a third of the continent's population, was largely believed to be supernatural. Religious scholars taught that death by pestilence was a martyrdom, assuring the believer's place in paradise. For non-believers, it was a punishment.

Until recently, for most of humanity, meaning in life was revealed through death, in the form of heaven, hell, or reincarnation. In the after-life, all would be revealed. Our earthly occupation was an opening act to the eternal life.

As science has uncovered the genuine physiological causes of death, our relationship to mortality has transformed. For better... and worse. It has become a human engineering problem. Death is no longer the providence of God, it's in the hands of doctors and scientists. As Yuval Harari posits, "when someone dies now, it's generally someone's fault."

We think of our current pandemic as a human mistake from its inception in Wuhan to our varying degrees of success in managing it worldwide.

And, of course, the generally accepted solution to the pandemic, the vaccine, is also squarely in human hands. While some may be praying in churches, synagogues and mosques, no one expects a pastor, in a moment of revelation, to pull a vaccine serum from behind the pulpit.

The development of the vaccine will take place in a lab by someone in white coat, not a Merlin's cap. It will be a product of human knowledge that we practically expect as part of our Amazon Prime membership.

The human fixation with the afterlife has significantly waned. In a very short period of time, from an evolutionary standpoint, we have re-framed the meaning of life into corporeal and ephemeral terms.

The harsh awareness of our own mortality has never been more acute. The global pandemic, replete with its archetypes and memes, has shone a blinding light on our impermanence—the Grim reaper clutching a scythe collecting souls on a Miami beach, images of desolate post-apocalyptic urban streets.

It's happening right here, right now, connected to our physiology.

Science has certainly done a better job than religion in being flexible, applying trial and error as a method for analysis. But there is danger in over-ascribing "meaning" to our limited and uncertain lifespan and to presuming that we have undue power over our mortality. We now live with a tremendous fear of death.

We marshal endless resources in keeping our elderly on life-support, despite terminal conditions, often leading to drawn-out, inhumane deaths. Our elders, once seen as the holders of ancient wisdom, are increasingly perceived as a burden, relegated to grim nursing homes.

Well-intentioned safety measures seemingly have no end. Charles Eisenstein addresses this idea eloquently in his article The Coronation.[1] No more diving boards, endless helmeting and belting, home security systems, and a general distrust of the natural world.

And, of course, now, in the fever pitch of our pandemic-induced hysteria, we incessantly scrub our hands, avoid touching our own faces and relegate social interactions to Zoom.

Certainly, for a short period, we must cohere as a society for our mutual benefit. We can and should wear face masks, elbow bump, and socially distance.

In the long term, however, on the other side of COVID, how much are we willing to sacrifice in life in an attempt to avert death?

Are we willing to shutter our community centers, our yoga studios, our temples for music, sport and culture?

Are we willing to succumb to a surveillance culture that tracks our every move and encounter?

Are we willing to give up on our own immune function?

Are we willing to strip the life out of life for the sake of life?

Despite all of the heart-wrenching suffering, the pandemic has offered humanity a pause for the re-assessment of life and death — and what makes them sacred.

What lies beyond, we cannot know. And we need to become more comfortable in this uncertainty lest we make our human experience miserable. Perhaps we can embrace death, not as a sanctimonious rebirth, but as a quiet return home.

Perhaps the solution is a shift from fear of death to a joy for life.

WRITING EXERCISES

Death comes to us in many forms, and none of us are immune. Reflect on the questions posed in this essay.

Describe your personal experiences with death, from the loss of loved ones and pets to other forms of death.

What thoughts and emotions arise when you contemplate your own death?

_____

_____

_____

_____

What small, tangible actions can you take that will help you shift from a fear of death to a joy for life, while still honoring health, well-being, and care for yourself and others?

_____

_____

_____

_____

Have your feelings about death evolved since Spring 2020? If so, in what ways?

_____

_____

_____

_____

_____

_____

FOR THOSE BATTLING IN PAPER ARMOR

MAY 24

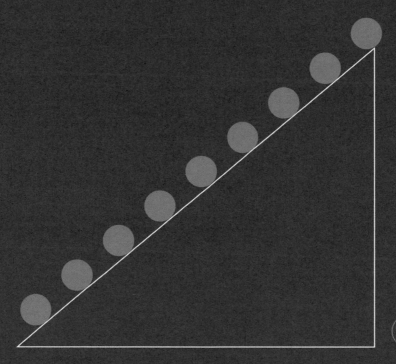

As restrictions around the country eased and all 50 states began to reopen, a subdued Memorial Day marked the unofficial start to summer, and many wondered if the heat would help deter the virus that had ravaged the country. The coronavirus death toll neared 100,000 as the first vaccine was tested, with positive results. Unemployment rates reached 20%, the highest since the Great Depression. Essential workers, predominantly people of color and migrants, found themselves continuing to suffer in low paying jobs as home care providers, delivery people, meatpacking and factory workers, often making less than $20,000 annually.

Tomorrow, in America, we celebrate Memorial Day. We pause to honor and mourn the men and women of our Armed forces who have died in service to our country.

However, in this twisted time, a new global war conscripts a different type of soldier, wearing a different sort of uniform. Instead of Army Greens, this infantry dons scrubs, aprons, Pullman Brown and Dickies denims.

They are caring for our forgotten elders, stocking shelves and delivering supplies. They are toiling in fields, factories and warehouses to ensure the nation's food chain functions. They are keeping our public transport on life support. They are nursing the ill and processing the dead.

This letter is an elegy to them.

The front lines are not the perilous, but fortified, desert camps. They are the subway tracks and outer-borough hospitals, the slaughterhouses and prisons, the distribution centers and grocery stores.

The heroism of this corps is not the glory stuff of Mandela and Chavez, though they are predominantly people of color. Their heroics are, instead, unheralded, nameless and fameless, fighting an invisible enemy that cannot be slain, only grimly flattened.

There is little grandeur to it. No medals. No Pomp and Circumstance. But, in this moment of collective heart-ache, they have kept us going. If vulnerability is synonymous with courage, then these folks are among history's bravest.

They have been dubbed "essential workers." Yet they are so under-resourced that Sujatha Gidla, a New York City subway conductor, describes her colleagues not as essential but as sacrificial. The list of those we now remember grows: Yolanda Woodberry, who worked as a bus driver in Philadelphia for 17 years; Rakkhon Kim, a letter carrier in the Bronx; Saul Sanchez, Eduardo Conchas de la Cruz and Tibursio Rivera López, who all worked at the same meatpacking plant in Colorado.

It begins with the explicit recognition that sanitation workers, emergency room nurses, grocery clerks and meatpackers have always been essential. They did not enlist for heroism nor court the grandiosity of the Blue Angels. In fact, in our hero worship, we risk absolving our own complicity in the atrocity of our structural failures.

As I type, I pull my Buff mask up over my stinging eyes in shame. The words of Gandhi haunt me, "the true measure of any society can be found in how it treats its most vulnerable members." How can we let this happen?

Memorial Day. Summer opens its doors. A white-walled Studebaker rolls down Main Street. Old Sergeant Murphy, the last of the Greatest Generation rides shotgun, waving a pint-sized flag. The band blares Sousa. The beach house is unshuttered. We take the wire brush to the barbecue. A flapping roadside balloon man touts a clearance sale at the local Ford dealer. No, not this year.

It is bleak but there is a greater calling.

How do we properly honor these heroes? Men and women who didn't enlist to be the bulwark against apocalyptical chaos, but nevertheless showed up for battle in paper armor.

We can value thoughts and prayers, a commemorative wreath and a trumpet's mournful Taps. But our hearts know this is not enough.

The lucky undrafted must undergo a deep moral inventory to determine how to fittingly exalt these inadvertent warriors, some of whom have made the ultimate sacrifice just by going to work.

It cannot be a mere gesture, a flimsy meme (or this insubstantial letter). Gratitude is the work and action we undertake that recognizes the gift that we have been given.

It begins with the explicit recognition that sanitation workers, emergency room nurses, grocery clerks and meatpackers have always been essential. They did not enlist for heroism nor court the grandiosity of the Blue Angels. In fact, in our hero worship, we risk absolving our own complicity in the atrocity of our structural failures.

What our essential workers desperately require is protective gear, a raise, comprehensive health care, proper sick leave, and organizations to advocate on their behalf.

They deserve access to well-being; movement, restoration and nutrition that reduce the conditions of comorbidity, stress and anxiety.

And, yes, they warrant the respect and support of our government, the most rudimentary return of their tax dollars.

If we are to honor them then we must demand that our leadership provide these basic needs and where they cannot, we must ask ourselves to furnish them where we can.

Patriotism is not protesting mask-wearing on the capital's steps. It is sacrificing so someone else's child you don't know in another state can have health insurance.

If there is any small tribute we can muster, it is to put aside our petty differences and individual material needs to find common decency, to better align our human condition with our highest principles.

For to honor the other is to honor the self, not only because we all share a divine nature, but because our very existence depends on them.

Let this Day of Remembrance draw upon the phantoms of our past and harness its pain to project a world that narrows the disparity of the human experience towards justice.

WRITING EXERCISES

When we acknowledge the sacrifice of others, we can begin to manifest the gratitude we feel into real action. Reflect on the sacrifices that you and others have had to make during the pandemic.

What sacrifices have you made? What sort of sacrifices have those in your community made? How do these sacrifices impact the world around you?

What principles are embodied in these sacrifices and why do you value them?

_____

_____

_____

_____

_____

_____

_____

_____

_____

_____

_____

_____

How can these same principles tangibly extend into your own life?

_____

_____

_____

_____

_____

_____

_____

_____

_____

_____

_____

_____

8 MINUTES, 46 SECONDS

MAY 31

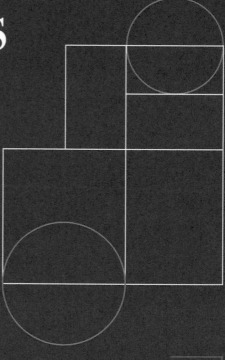

On May 25, 2020, Minneapolis police officer Derek Chauvin killed George Floyd, a Black man, by pinning him to the ground, with his knee on his neck, as the suffocating man repeatedly said, "I can't breathe." A video of the incident quickly went viral and thousands took to the streets of Minneapolis in the following days. Protests and clashes with police intensified after prosecutors refrained from charging any of the police officers involved in the killing. Police used tear gas, along with rubber bullets, against the protesters. Dozens of buildings, including a police precinct, were set on fire. Rioting and looting escalated, and the president mobilized the National Guard in many cities. Unrest spread across the country, with tens of thousands flooding the streets of US cities including Los Angeles, Memphis, Louisville, Atlanta, Detroit, Philadelphia, and New York. Throughout 2020, accounts of police brutality towards black people continued to surface, adding to anger over racial disparity, and disproportionate data showing that black people are 3x more likely to contract COVID-19, 2x more likely to die from the virus, and disproportionately make up the essential workforce.

It's late Saturday night. There's a curfew in place here in Los Angeles. Hours ago, police discharged rubber bullets and pepper spray at protestors on Fairfax, less than 2 miles from here. I feel a mix of fury, confusion, guilt, powerlessness and a rare uncertainty about what to do. I sense I am not alone.

In college, I concentrated in race relations. I remember studying Robert F. Kennedy's extemporaneous eulogy for Martin Luther King as he consoled a bereaved crowd in Indianapolis on the evening of his assassination. It moved me to tears. He invoked Aeschylus:

"And even in our sleep, pain that cannot forget falls drop by drop upon the heart, and in our own despair, against our will, comes wisdom, by the awful grace of God."

Over half a century later, we still await the wisdom that is the promise of this pain. Again, in unbearable heartache, we are left to wonder just how long is the arc of the moral universe.

We have all seen it now. 8 minutes and 46 seconds of knee on neck. Rodney King haunts this moment. The embers from the fires in South Central have smoldered in our country over the past quarter century, fed by the videos that expose the epidemic of police brutality against African Americans.

While deeply retraumatizing, especially for the Black community, the widespread sharing of footage on social media has sparked public outrage, launched civic protest, and led to legal action. But it has not increased accountability in most police departments or slowed these savage slayings.

Walter Scott. Eric Harris, Trayvon Martin, Eric Garner. Freddie Gray, Michael Brown. Philando Castile. Breonna Taylor, Ahmaud Arbery, George Floyd and scores more.

As fires burn in Minneapolis, we ask what fire burns in the hearts of men that stokes such anger as to take another's life? What heavy smoke

Man is not born with this rage. It is learned. And the slaughter of innocent African-Americans will not end until we engage in a deep personal and societal moral inventory that isn't resolved simply by bringing assailants to justice but by addressing the roots of this societal rage. What are the cultural conditions that lead white men to brutalize black men? It may be the most complicated historical question Americans will ever confront.

clouds a man's moral judgment to deny another's breath: breath that is our birthright, repeated 23,000 times a day without thought, and taken away, in a brutal moment, without thought?

Man is not born with this rage. It is learned. And the slaughter of innocent African-Americans will not end until we engage in a deep personal and societal moral inventory that isn't resolved simply by bringing assailants to justice but by addressing the roots of this societal rage. What are the cultural conditions that lead white men to brutalize black men? It may be the most complicated historical question Americans will ever confront.

Swinging between outrage and numbness, we are left wondering what to do.

Words. Do they matter? Of course, they do. King reminds us, "In the end, we will remember not the words of our enemies, but the silence of our friends."

Speak out, we must. But, before we do, find the silent reflection that Derek Chauvin could not, for that is God's only voice. Let our words articulate a clarity and moral authority that reflects this quietness, as if our prayer cushion lay across the bare floor of a Birmingham jail.

As a white person, I am seeking to find my appropriate place in this wickedness. If you are white, be humble and listen. But do not be inhibited in your humility lest your silence be complicit in this injustice. For just as a man can transcend self regardless of his religion, so can a man find truth irrespective of his skin color.

But what to do when words feel so inadequate? When they cannot extinguish the agony and frustration that flares in our hearts.

Take to the street and pray with our feet?

Our social contract demands that we relinquish certain rights such that we receive greater rights and protections. But when society is in breach, when a people are not in receipt of those protections, is not civil disobedience justifiable?

We are left with the same tough questions etched by Langston Hughes in 1951:

What happens to a dream deferred?

> Does it dry up
> like a raisin in the sun?
> Or fester like a sore—
> And then run?
> Does it stink like rotten meat?
> Or crust and sugar over—
> like a syrupy sweet?
>
> Maybe it just sags
> like a heavy load.
>
> *Or does it explode?*

Right now, it feels explosive. Right now, the Dream feels so far away. The real dream is, of course, that the Dream is no longer a dream.

We must do all we can, every one of us, to instantiate a reality that extends all the protections and opportunities guaranteed in our mutual national contract to *everyone*. This must start with ourselves, but also extend into every nook of humanity.

What can you do?

Honestly examine your implicit biases and change them. Read and educate yourself. See your personal wellness as inextricably tied with the well-being of society.

Hold your lawmakers accountable. Foster and energize your community. Stand up, march, speak out. Talk to your kids, and your parents, and your neighbors. Listen a lot. Become an activist in the way that is authentic to you – whether that is quiet and empathic or loud and bold.

The world is not something happening to you. You are an active participant in the human condition.

Maya Angelou wrote, "History, despite its wrenching pain cannot be unlived, but if faced with courage, need not be lived again." May we both pray and work for the dawning of a new morning.

For additional resources, please see the index in the back of the book.

WRITING EXERCISES

The killing of George Floyd and the Movement for Black Lives impacted everyone in different ways. Reflecting back on this time may be retraumatizing so please make sure that you are in a suitable headspace to revisit these issues.

What was the emotional impact of watching the video of George Floyd's murder? How did it make you feel?

What judgments did you make about Mr. Floyd, Mr. Chauvin and the other policemen who were there?

_____

_____

_____

_____

_____

Regardless of your race, how have you navigated your desire (or lack thereof) to speak out?

_____

_____

_____

_____

_____

_____

_____

_____

How have you balanced the conflicting needs to express yourself and listen?

_____

_____

_____

_____

_____

_____

_____

_____

_____

THE BOILING POINT

JUNE 7

Black Lives Matter protests continued in the wake of George Floyd's death, making it one of the largest movements in history. Over half a million people protested in the streets on June 6th in over 500 locations across the country. While protests remained peaceful during the day, many cities instituted curfews, arresting those who were out after dark. At the same time, the US reached 2 million confirmed coronavirus cases and 112,000 deaths from the virus, with surges reaching states like Texas, Arizona and Florida. In Washington, protesters in Lafayette Square were dispersed with tear-gas to clear the way for a presidential photo-op in front of a church. In cities across the country President Trump dispatched the National Guard, along with almost a dozen other federal forces and unidentified federal officers, to "dominate" protesters. Meanwhile, the Minneapolis City Council promised to dismantle the police force.

The kettle is whistling. The water is roiling. Why now?

What takes a simmer to a boil?

On Tuesday, muted in solidarity, I called my friend Anasa. She bears no responsibility to answer my queries or hold my shaking hand. Yet she gives me two full hours of her self; her story, her wisdom, her grace. As I listen it becomes evident that, despite studying race relations in college, my true understanding of the African-American experience is a speck on a pinhead.

This is what sinks in when you take one day to shut the hell up and listen:

The fire under this kettle was lit as soon as The White Lion[2] dropped anchor. The heat has been relentless for Black Americans ever since, but over the last three months, the burner has ratcheted up under the entire country. The murder of George Floyd, the final 212th degree.

The coronavirus was the first layer of tinder, revealing the stark inequality and the fragility of the safety net for African-Americans.

Black Americans are 2.5 times more likely to die from the pandemic than White Americans. In Illinois, African-Americans make up 15% of the population and 42% of the deaths. In Chicago, 30% of the population and 72% of the deaths. Those statistics[3] hold true everywhere. Why?

African-Americans predominantly live in poor and dense urban areas, which makes social distancing impossible. They often suffer from pre-existing conditions, making them susceptible to serious reactions to the virus. This co-morbidity has its roots in the inaccessibility of nutritious food and quality health care. The jobs available to African-Americans do not frequently offer health insurance but, ironically, often pay too much to qualify for Medicaid. The kettle simmers.

Dire health outcomes were compounded by the fact that many Black Americans do not have a reserve of savings to buffer sudden unemployment. Unemployment for Black Americans was 6.7% in March. Now, it

Protests set against the backdrop of COVID-19, still stealing a thousand American lives daily, presents an agonizing choice: What takes primacy: righteous passive resistance or public health? This pathogen will surely spread through the spraying passion of those of us gathered tightly on city streets. The willingness to protest, despite the virus, reflects the depth of public rage.

is 16.8%, stressing households already on the brink. The token relief of federal funding was not equitably distributed to black businesses, as PPP funding went primarily to businesses with established banker relationships. Despite Friday's surprisingly positive job report, black unemployment ticked upward. Often last hired and first fired, less than half of black adults now have a job.[4] The water bubbles.

And then, on Monday, May 25, the world witnessed the brutal murder of George Floyd. Just one more in a seemingly endless litany of brutalities against African Americans — but this time, steam jets out the spout.

The wicked triptych of the pandemic – with its disproportionate impact, persistent economic disadvantage intensified by unemployment, and a chronic militarism brought into stark relief in Minneapolis – opened the floodgates. And folks poured out into the streets.

Protests set against the backdrop of COVID-19, still stealing a thousand American lives daily, presents an agonizing choice: What takes primacy: righteous passive resistance or public health? This pathogen will surely spread through the spraying passion of those of us gathered tightly on city streets. The willingness to protest, despite the virus, reflects the depth of public rage.

But, of course, many Black Americans were never working remotely. They are disproportionally the bus and subway drivers, sanitation workers and meatpackers, grocery and convenience store clerks, nurses and delivery people. Not only do Black Americans bear the brunt of the epidemic of police brutality, they are also the most exposed to the viral pandemic because they are, and always have been, among America's essential workers.

In the last 13 days, we have collectively spiraled through myriad emotions: anger, frustration, despair, uncertainty. But in this emotional murk, a ray of hope shimmers, spurring us forward.

This passion is being channeled into a level of civic engagement unseen in half a century. Thousands have joined in increasingly peaceful and patriotic protest. A significant number of white people are pausing to take moral inventory and examine their responsibility and accountability for the racism endemic to our country. The pandemic, which forced many to look inwards in a reassessment of priorities, has kindled a mass expression of renewed moral clarity.

This broad coalition has inspired global demonstrations of solidarity, reminding us of what made America great in the first place. When we are at our best, we inspire the world.

In this tumult, we ask, "What now? What can we draw from the past?"

A humble prayer:

If you are protesting, you are the face of the movement. If you do not assail, the movement becomes morally unassailable.

If you wear blue, consider that those taking a knee seek to protect others from a knee. The communities that most need your protection and service may also be the people you see marching in the street. This may be frustrating and require compassion. In this compassion, trust is built.

If you are white, now is a time to learn, grow, donate and serve. Meditate in the discomfort of sitting outside the circle. Be humble in solidarity, but never silent in complicity. Leverage your privilege and platforms in support of justice beyond performative allyship.

This will be a battle both of and for hearts and minds. It will be dramatic and dull, rebellious and systemic. The broadcasting of continued police brutality and political venality that equally horrifies and inspires us, rests upon the structural and banal: The denied loan, rebuffed application, redlined district, passed-over promotion and rejected offer. It is rooted in a privatized prison system that incarcerates 20% of black men, two-thirds of whom have not been convicted of any crime but cannot afford bail.

The challenge must be met with inspired oratory, peaceful protest, activist art and civil disobedience: actions that shine a light on injustice and demand attention. But this effort will fall short, as President Obama recently wrote, if there is not systemic, legislative and institutional change both at the federal and the local level, where most police and criminal justice reform takes place. Let many march in the streets in June so that we ALL march to the polls in November.

When leadership is as deaf as justice is blind, when it bunkers away only to emerge viciously as a false prophet, then who raises her hand to lead?

Are you ready?

Are you willing not just to answer the call, but also answer the calls? Right the wrongs and write the laws? Pray with your heart and with your feet?

It will take a village to build a global one. Pastors and web designers, community organizers and speech writers, meditation teachers and loan officers, secretaries and bail bondsmen, lawyers and civil servants, health care workers and a vice president.

If you want in, there's a role for you, however you can authentically show up.

The water is boiling. The kettle is screaming.

Will it evaporate? Will it just condensate? Or worse, will it burn?

Or will this steam, which when harnessed powers the locomotive and riverboat, propel us towards justice?

There is work to do. Finally, it feels like it is up to us.

WRITING EXERCISES

Most of us share the vision of racial equity. We are frustrated and angered when we witness injustice and that exasperation may overflow onto our social media pages or in animated debates with friends. Even though these expressions are rooted in good intentions, they often do not translate into real change or progress.

Take a moment to reflect on the things you can do in your own life, however large or small, to instantiate a more just and equitable world.

PRIVILEGE

JUNE 14

It's hot.

Schuyler, my three daughters and I walk east on DeLongpre to the protest.

Others are clamoring down the street, placards in hand, engaged in various forms of spirited horseplay. A sort of nervous energy pervades, like one that precedes performance. It is Hollywood after all.

I am tuned out, lost in thought, moated in the subjective experience of what it is to be me. My mind chatters on incessantly, as it has for weeks, commentating on my blundering internal investigation into where and how I am complicit in the oppression of a people who have so deeply shaped who I am.

I have never been blind to the obvious and insidious crimes of racism in America, nor my role as accomplice. But I assumed there was a fluidity to my identity because my formative years were so inextricably tied to Black musicians, writers, politicians and athletes.

As I kid, I spent the better of ten thousand hours sweating buckets in my dad's attic, learning the repertoire of Reverend Gary Davis and Mississippi John Hurt on the guitar. I had this tape recorder that played half speed. I would rewind over and over a hundred times to get it right. I burned through Waller, Ellington, Strayhorn, Ella, Miles, Canonball, Billie, Monk, Nina, Herbie, Benson. Transcribed Wes, which was nearly impossible. In my 20's, like everyone else, I wanted to be like Mike, watching TBS all night to grok every nuance of his post moves, the little lean he did to create just enough space. Those who know, know. And my moral universe, shaped through the oratory of King and Obama and the prose of Angelou and Morrison. Passages I practiced in front of the mirror and turns of phrase that I yearn to echo here.

Now I wonder if I can no longer authentically claim this part of myself. Is white hero worship of African Americans an inverted form of oppression? Or is it an expression of the best of humanity, one individual's celebration of another's brilliance?

What I do know is that the distance between who constitutes my cultural personhood and who constitutes the corporate boards I sit on and the student body of my children's schools are as wide as the desert sky.

It's hot. As we wind through the city, my moral inventory winds on, too.

My loving grandparents, whose commitment to America and the promise of its dream, put family in front of self. It is they who assured my education, who gave generously to charity, who, themselves, emerged from oppression; yet what were the derogatory slurs they uttered under their breath?

What implicit biases lurk inside me? What false narratives of history have sculpted my identity?

Where the world shapes the self, what are the devious forces that imprint our character? And what patterns must be unwound so that the self can better shape the world?

Sure, I am deeply committed to aligning my works and actions on this planet with my highest principles. I am generally kind, compassionate and generous. Yet, have I once honestly considered the benefits that I have accrued; that every loan application I've submitted has been approved, every insurance policy granted, that I haven't been pulled over in thirty years?

I am sitting in the dissonance that you can be a good person and fully complicit in the structures and systems that have ravaged a people and denied them equal rights, protections and opportunities.

Of course, this moment is not about me. And yet, it is about every single one of us. Which is exactly why we are straddling the potential of true generational shift. Which way shall we march?

As we approach the Hollywood precinct on Wilcox, police outposts pop up stirring agitation among the scattered groups of activists. I am shepherding my flock north across the street when I catch the eye of an African American cop. My heart lurches in my chest as it imagines being Black and blue in this moment, bruised by a competing fealty between race and colleague. Instinctively, I give him a short, deliberate salute, a feeble attempt at empathy. He nods, gently.

Where the world shapes the self, what are the devious forces that imprint our character? And what patterns must be unwound so that the self can better shape the world?

We roll up to Vine from Sunset. The crowd thickens here from every angle as if the tributaries of the Nile, Yangtze, Amazon, Ganges and Mississippi are all emptying into one global ocean.

Signs of every imaginable size and tenor are held proudly aloft like an Olympics ceremony. Koreans for Black Lives. Latinas for Black Lives. LGBTQIA for Black Lives.

Even Spidermen for Black Lives. There's a reason why it's lovingly dubbed Hollyweird by its local denizens. The assortment of superheroes assimilates seamlessly as, of course, we are all wearing masks.

This twisted but hopeful moment in history has tightly crammed 20,000 people together in the midst of a viral pandemic, the size of the crowd directly proportional to the depth of the frustration.

Multitudes are infilling behind us but the front is not moving, packing us ever more tightly, like a pumped and untapped keg (of Corona? not funny, I know). There's a restless buzzing as the electrons of our outer shells begin to bond, unifying us.

It's hot.

Finally, we're moving. The drums begin beating. The crowd starts chanting, a full-throated call and response. No Justice. No Peace. No Justice. No Peace. Say his name. George Floyd. Say her name. Breonna Taylor. A mighty, rag-tag chorus of humanity.

Left on Yucca.

There's not a single barricade yet a collective intelligence knows the way. Not a single uniform, yet everyone peaceful. People sweating and hungry are getting tossed free water and snacks, a pop-up gift economy based on need, not greed. There's no one making money here. No VIP section. No side door. No laminate.

Just a sea of humanity, singing effusively. And, in a moment, I am a wave swept up into the ocean deep. There is no me, only the world. No conscious thought, just being. No I, only we.

If you are Christian, you might interpret this sort of experience as the oneness of God. If you are Buddhist, it might be a glance into nirvana, a transcendence of self and a sensation of emptiness. If you are Hindu, you could associate this state with Brahman, a connection to the eternal self of which our individual consciousness is a mere variation. My only association with this state is the rarest deep meditation where I feel outside of my own body.

It is in these epiphanous moments that the utter absurdity of racism, or any form of separation, is revealed. In this unveiling of the illusory self, it is less that we are equal, which assumes our individuation, and more that we are one.

> *I am sitting in the dissonance that you can be a good person and fully complicit in the structures and systems that have ravaged a people and denied them equal rights, protections and opportunities.*

I don't pretend to know God, but divine faith may be the recognition that we are all connected by a power greater than us. And I sense God is more interested in us loving each other than He is in us loving Him.

Of course, our human experience with its structural and systemic fuckery is light years away from this exalted state but to glimpse it is to know what is possible.

Left on Ivar.

I am jolted back into the material world by a low flying drone. There's a hapless couple with two small babies in a minivan, which they clearly parked without any knowledge of an impending march. Even they are dancing in their seats.

We spill out on to Hollywood Boulevard which offers a wider berth and the intensity ratchets slightly down. There is an old Chrysler that has managed to wedge its way into the procession. A fabulously bejeweled young Black woman is perched on the door with her torso out the window tossing granola bars.

She spots little Micah, diminutive for her age, with her big Black Lives Matter poster held high.

"How old are you sweetheart?" she hollers.

"I'm 10!"

"What's a 10-year old doing out here caring about Black lives?" Her tone is playful and kind.

The edges of Micah's mask turn up. She feels seen.

The woman smiles at me, a distillation of grace.

I guide my estrogen footprint down McCadden Place, a side street shortcut to where our car is stationed. We peel away from the throng, back into the story of separation, where we are again just strangers living among other strangers in some crooked external universe.

I corral my kids into my car to return to my house.

It's hot. I crack the window and turn on the 1619 podcast and drive away.

What a privilege.

This essay explores my attempts to come to terms with my own privilege as a white person. However, privilege can be applied to gender, sexual orientation, ethnicity, social class, body type and other qualities. Take some time and reflect on how your identity relates to your privilege in society.

In what ways do society's systems and structure benefit you over someone else?

What is the history that has granted you this privilege?

_____
_____
_____
_____
_____
_____
_____
_____
_____
_____
_____
_____

What are some tangible actions you can take in the acknowledgement of your privilege that may help to realize a more equitable world?

_____
_____
_____
_____
_____
_____
_____
_____
_____
_____
_____
_____

FINDING
FATHERHOOD

JUNE 21

My father raised my brother and me through our teenage years as a single dad. It was not a course we chose, but one we maplessly navigated. Our relationship was hardly traditional, swinging between a pizza-for-breakfast kind of bromance and a deep loving co-dependency. As I stumbled into manhood and he, sometimes adolescently, rebuilt his life, we leaned into each other. We relished each other's company and shared a passion for the cocktail of music, politics and parties. Oh... the parties.

Eventually, somewhat against our will, adulthood beckoned. Time has a father as well. I sailed off into the wide berth of life as if I was the first one to attempt to distill it into meaning. When we're young, we don't know that God, that celestial Father, is right where we are.

Last year, my father was diagnosed with colon cancer. In the aftermath of his surgery, he lost 35 pounds and became very weak. He remained astonishingly sanguine through the ordeal but his voice, normally round, plump with eloquence, was serrated and fragile. I would often steer the daily conversations I had with him toward the empirical; the test results, the probabilities of metastasis, alternatives to chemotherapy. In the prosaic and scientific, it was easier to keep a stiff upper lip. All the tropes of traditional masculinity applied: My family needed me to remain strong, confident, armed with facts. Clad in emotional armor, I fought to maintain order and stability. The truth was, I thought I might lose him.

My middle daughter, Lolli, is an empath. She disappears for long periods of time by herself. One day, in the nadir of my dad's travails, I slumped into her room, lay on the bed next to her where she was reading and I began to cry. Not a whimper. A full-bellied, snotty-nosed, pillow-drenching sob. She held me tightly for a long time, nursing me out of convulsions. Generously breaking the silence, she said finally, "I guess big boys do cry."

Before I had kids, I had three theories on fatherhood. Now I have three kids and no theories. When you walk down the aisle of a bookstore, there are hundreds of tomes on fatherhood, which indicates there's no one right way to do it, no playbook. We're still finding it.

But what I know, for me, is that to be a good father, I need a wholesale re-examination of the typical male archetype.

It's not that the norms of manhood; courage, discipline and pride are, in and of themselves, bad. It is the stereotypical depiction of these qualities that are obsolete and misguided.

We have lucidly witnessed, both individually and as a nation, how the penchant to be a "real" man, with its chest-thumping hubris and social dominance, leads outwardly to bullying, misogyny and homophobia and inwardly to stress and depression. As men, and particularly as fathers, we have a choice to eschew this toxicity that is passed along down generational lines.

Can we redirect pride from an obsession with one's own excellence to a sense of contentment derived from another's fulfillment of their own potential?

Can we consider courage as synonymous with vulnerability, for seldom do they exist without each other? I know Lolli finds me brave, not because I can suppress a tear but because I can shed one.

Can we comprehend discipline as not solely the doling of punishment, but as a discipleship to our highest principles? Can we practice a familial form of restorative justice that focuses less on the punitive and more on addressing the harm caused?

If fathers and families can instantiate these practices in the home then will this not be reflected in the greater world? Would humanity not be more empathetic and compassionate?

When our family first relocated to Los Angeles, my daughters felt uprooted. This was particularly difficult for my eldest, Phoebe, who had cultivated meaningful friendships in Brooklyn. Right as she started sixth grade at her new school, there was an overnight science trip to the desert. The first afternoon, I got a call from the teacher. Phoebe was miserable and wanted to come home. I told her to give it some time. An hour later, the teacher called again and put Phoebe on the line. She was sobbing inconsolably. Of course, I felt for her. The notion of driving three hours there and back was daunting. I let her bawl until she was tired and then said, "If you want me to, I will come and get you right now.

And I won't make you feel guilty about it. Take twenty minutes and call back if you want me to come." Needless to say, the phone never rang. I learned something about fatherhood; provide support and give choice.

My girls are light years from perfect. They can be petty, spoiled and irreverent, mouthing their rendition of the Lord's Prayer, "Our father, who art in the carport, hollowed be his wallet. Please give us our daily bread, preferably in tens, and forgive us our debts. Lead us not into your woo-woo meditations, but deliver us from soccer."

Baldwin was right. They rarely listen to me, but they also rarely fail to imitate me. I have never once asked them to do their homework, yet they are exemplary students, perhaps because they witness me working diligently on this computer and in the yard and have internalized diligence as a virtue.

What else are our sons and daughters modeling from our examples – good and bad?

I am not confident that most fathers truly realize the extent of their influence and the degree to which our children crave our admiration. Nor, I suspect, does society truly comprehend the devastating impact of tearing fathers from their families, an issue we must immediately confront.

If we have any hope of advancing as a species – of ending war and eradicating racism - fathers must commit to an evolved paternity that shuns domineering patriarchy. We can hone our ability to share, cooperate, learn, follow and, very occasionally, ask for directions.

I send my father my weekly missive regularly for edits. Of course, what I really seek is his approval which he freely and proudly gives. He is doing well now. Just a bit embarrassed that a million people are reading about his colon. I suppose it's good for him. Fathers must be humble, too.

WRITING EXERCISES

Relationships with fathers are complicated and different for everone. Take some time to reflect and write about your father or about fatherhood generally. Perhaps recount a story that represents a certain aspect of his character. Think about what traits a good father embodies.

Sketch out some of the earliest memories that you have of your father. Use all of your physical senses. Describe the emotions that you feel when thinking about him.

_____

_____

_____

_____

_____

_____

_____

_____

_____

_____

Recount a story about your own father. Which of his traits are most prevalent in this story?

_____

_____

_____

_____

_____

_____

_____

_____

_____

_____

_____

_____

_____

Describe how you see your father reflected in you.

_____

_____

_____

_____

_____

What are/were the qualities of your father that you love/loved? That you hate/hated?

_____

_____

_____

_____

_____

_____

_____

Do you carry any of these qualities into your own life? Which ones?

_____

_____

_____

_____

If you're a father (or married to one), what are the best qualities that you or he embodies?
If you're not a father (or married to one), what advice might you give to the fathers of
the world?

_____

_____

_____

_____

_____

_____

WORDS MATTER

JUNE 28

In early April, during the depths of the *first* quarantine, Phoebe had a series of Vesuvian eruptions, the kind only a teenager can unleash; limbs flailing, snot spraying like lava spouts. Apparently, the Coronavirus was a pox sent specifically to destroy her life, and we were the worst parents in human history. My prompt for clarification about whether she was referring specifically to homo sapiens or any human species was not warmly received. These tantrums, punctuated by accusations of neglect and threats of self-harm, were both frightening and perplexing. Finally, she would flame out, like one of those extra-long fireplace matches, her tall frame crumbling on the bed like ash.

After a few explosive weeks, we boiled the kettle and convened as a family on the patio. We talked and listened for two hours. The early parental refrain, "use your words, honey," never really loses utility.

In the calm embrace of chamomile, Phoebe found her words, channeling emotions into sentences. She felt disempowered, enraged and despairing. There seemed to be no end in sight for the shoddy online schooling, the loneliness of social isolation, cancelled plans, and way too much nuclear family.

These acute pressures are suspended on a continuous cortisol drip of worry over climate catastrophe and societal unraveling. Our children have a low-level sense of impending doom, one that I never had as an adolescent chasing balls on various courts. This spectre of Armageddon contributes to a wanton recklessness, often summed up with a flippant "What does it matter anyways? The world is going to end."

We learned that COVID had stripped Phoebe of what she relies on to maintain a semblance of equanimity; the symbiosis of friendship. Love her as we do, we can't provide that for her. She finds a solace and shared identity that can be only accessed through her contemporaries. I suppose, we all do.

After a lengthy dissertation on germ theory and social distancing - which, to her credit, Phoebe respectfully indulged - we devised a way for her to merge bubbles with her best friend after they had both quarantined for two weeks.

We created space. She found words as vessels for her feelings. From words, conversation sprung forth. And through conversation, we understood each other and found common ground. The simple is often so hard.

Dialogue is not just a healthy recipe for families.

In many ways, society is having a tantrum right now. We are screaming over each other. Black Lives Matter. All Lives Matter. Wear a mask. COVID is over. Defund the Police. Law & Order.

Indeed, now is the time to step boldly into our civic responsibilities and fight for our convictions, to shorten the arc of the moral universe. At the same time, liberal democracy is predicated on pluralism, a tolerance for a multiplicity of ideas. We need to cultivate public forums for the free, thoughtful exchange of ideas among individuals, such that moral virtue can cream to the top.

Brené Brown says, "People are hard to hate close up. Move in."

It can be awkward and painful to engage directly with those who we see as adversaries, but these are the exchanges that will truly tip the balance for universal principles. And even when we are tempted to scream on Facebook, can we find the words and the grace to imagine that we are truly face-to-face? To both listen and make our best and most thoughtfully researched case?

Social media is without doubt an incredible organizing tool. But how can we communicate if we don't actually talk to one another?

Cosider the recent rulings by the Supreme Court in favor of LGBTQ rights and the preservation of DACA. The Court can certainly be swayed by political loyalty and there are other significant judgments with which I do not agree. However, the assent for the majority in the Title VII case that protects gay and transgender people in the workplace was written by Neil Gorsuch, a conservative jurist appointed by this administration. This rare modern example of moral clarity taking primacy over political affiliation may not have been possible without the traditions of the Supreme Court, arguably one of the last vestiges of thorough and respectful debate. Indeed, the adjudication of the case itself turned on a nuanced interpretation of the words, "because of sex."

The power of expansive conversation can bend people's ideological predispositions.

Indeed, now is the time to step boldly into our civic responsibilities and fight for our convictions, to shorten the arc of the moral universe. At the same time, liberal democracy is predicated on pluralism, a tolerance for a multiplicity of ideas. We need to cultivate public forums for the free, thoughtful exchange of ideas among individuals, such that moral virtue can cream to the top.

The atomization and polarization of our society has been intensified by social media, the primary forum through which we "connect." In a world largely devoid of religious affiliation and hazy national fealty, social media provides us with the opportunity to express our individual "political" identity. And it's powerful — but dangerous. Our individual humanity is nuanced and complex. And social media, a strange non-consensual psychological experiment, radically tests our inter-relatedness. How can we properly express our identity or deeply held beliefs in 280 characters or less? Is it no wonder that we're just hollering in an echo-chamber? Ask yourself, would you make that comment if that person was sitting across the table? Is social media expression predominantly private acts happening in public?

The posting of mawkish quote cards and viral memes (of which I am admittedly guilty) are often, at best, performative and, at worst, amplifications of unexcavated ideas. Science and media are imperfect institutions, but they are founded on traditions of rigor. And when they are systemically undermined, when there is no objective or even inter-subjective fact grounding us in a shared understanding of 'reality,' we all become easy prey to the hysteria of the moment. It becomes tantalizing to post wobbly notions of conspirituality. How many of us are guilty of posting a meme or slogan and becoming a vector for an idea that we don't completely understand? I've surely done it.

Consider, for example, Defund the Police. On the surface, to some, it feels potentially radical and divisive. Without investigation, the slogan might suggest the complete abandonment of law enforcement, which some do support. But once this policy is thoroughly unpacked and discussed, there is so much common ground to share. Why should police be dealing with the mentally ill, managing domestic disputes or doling out parking tickets? Who could outright reject the reallocation of funding to address homelessness and drug addiction? Whatever your political persuasion, isn't there a conversation here?

The human species is unique in that we can cooperate at scale through the exchange of words. It is communication that has thrust us to the top of the food chain, and its dearth that can transmute us into warring locust swarms. Words matter so much right now.

Further, if we took the time to learn the history of American policing and mass incarceration from militias to slave patrols, from the "professionalization" of police post-Prohibition to Nixon's Southern strategy, from Rockefeller drug laws to the War on Drugs, from the Crime Bill to mandatory minimum sentences, from three strikes to the privatization of prisons; If we had a honest and meticulous discussion about policing and criminal justice, I cannot believe that 95% of people would not believe in wholesale reform.

This is not about gradualism, it is about a systemic change that requires words to both inspire and write law.

This is not about compromising beliefs, it's about committing to them so deeply that you are willing to bear them witness.

This is not about arming yourself with vitriolic barbs, it is about fortifying yourself with unassailable rigor.

If we have any hope of actually communicating with one another, the words we use matter.

Call me a dreamer, but I haven't given up on people's intrinsic goodness and flexibility. I simply believe that enough of us need to find the patience and the words to have the brave thorny conversations.

The human species is unique in that we can cooperate at scale through the exchange of words. It is communication that has thrust us to the top of the food chain, and its dearth that can transmute us into warring locust swarms. Words matter so much right now.

Seismic upheaval often cultivates fertile ground for deep connection. The soulversation we had with Phoebe in April was the outgrowth of jarring emotional tectonics. What makes a family work also makes a society work. These past 4 months (perhaps 4 years) have been raw and challenging, with hope and despair pulling at both ends of a frayed lace. But don't we all feel the portent of a generational moment?

Can we sit down around millions of tables, digital and wooden, to speak from the heart and listen with the soul? It's a tall order. But the alternative looks like a nation of teenagers on a bender. What stands between us and the world our hearts know is possible may be thousands of knotty thoughtful conversations.

WRITING EXERCISES

Overwhelm and the inability to communicate our feelings are common and shared human experiences.

Was there a time during 2020 that you felt so overwhelmed by emotion that you weren't able to convey what you were really thinking or feeling?

_____

_____

Can you go back to that moment and try to describe it with words now?

_____

_____

_____

_____

_____

_____

_____

_____

_____

_____

_____

_____

_____

_____

_____

_____

_____

_____

6.28

Are there certain topics that are easy for you to speak and write about?
Which ones are the most difficult?

_____

_____

_____

_____

_____

_____

_____

_____

_____

_____

Think of a time when you brought up a sticky issue with a friend, family member
or stranger. What happened? Is there something you wish you could have said?

_____

_____

_____

_____

_____

_____

_____

_____

_____

_____

_____

_____

INTERDEPENDENCE DAY
JULY 5

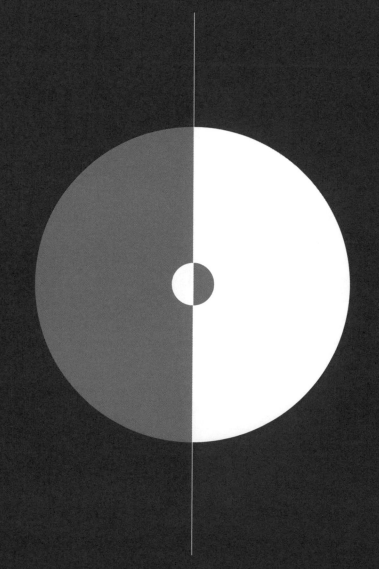

I am in my happy place, snug in the middle lane of the 101 coasting at a modest 60 miles per hour, listening to The Daily, driving to Topanga with Micah. Schuyler thinks I drive too slowly. I prefer "cautious." It might be genetic.

My beloved Nana, barely 5 feet in heels, seldom broke 25 on the speedometer. As a young boy, I would often accompany her to her sacred weekly hairdresser appointment. There was a soda fountain there in which I enthusiastically indulged, creating madcap papercup cocktails of Mr. Pibb and Fanta. Eventually, she'd emerge from the chair, grip my hand, her long glossy red nails digging at my forearm skin, and lead me out to the mini-mall parking lot.

Automobiles did not spare steel in the 1970's. Nana would board her colossal Cadillac, often unwittingly parked askew across two spots, like a mouse saddling an elephant. She didn't drive it as much as it drove her. She'd crawl out of the lot into traffic like a cruise liner leaving port, eyes peering out underneath the top curve of the wheel, nothing but her fabulous frosted red coiffure visible to leery fellow drivers. She would retell the same yarn of her father's arrival at Ellis Island and then improvise with Ethel Merman schmaltz, "Only in America." We'd stop to get Carvel. Heaven.

Generally, one podcast episode perfectly fills my commute to Topanga. Fourth of July weekend approaches and host Michael Barbaro is reciting our founding doctrine from our greatest piece of American literature. We know it almost too well, like a prayer uttered so many times that we forget its meaning:

"We hold these truths to be self-evident, that all men are created equal, that they are endowed by their Creator, with certain inalienable rights, that among these are Life, Liberty and the pursuit of Happiness."

This lofty egalitarian ideal is the plot line of our national mythology. In its time, it was a radical repudiation of feudal European pre-destiny, where you were born either into aristocracy or serfdom and there you remained. This Declaration dispensed with the divine right of kings, ushered in the Enlightenment and anointed individuals with the power to choose their own government.

Of course, we know this national folklore has been so often a fairytale, a false narrative. Just because these rights were scrawled on a parchment did not mean they came for free. Generation after generation, passionately engaged citizens have waged principled battles to better align our human condition with our most cherished principles. And, again, this call beckons.

When the framers penned the notion of all men as equal, they were certainly not drawing from evolutionary biology. A Darwinian understanding of the world was a century away and, of course, from a genetic perspective, we are all snowflakes. The concept of equality was based in the spiritual, specifically in the Judeo-Christian notion that every person is born with an eternal soul judged equally before God.

Yet, in the same stanza of this Declaration, there is a paradox. The spiritual notion of a land of equals striving for a common good echoed eleven years later in our Constitution by "We the people," "a common defense," "general welfare," "more perfect union" and "United" states exists in stark contrast with inalienable individual entitlements. Life, liberty and the pursuit of happiness have become increasingly applied to sanctifying the rights of the individual and protecting the ability to own property and amass material wealth. How we square our commonality and individualism has always engendered fierce national debate.

This tug of war between the common good and individual rights, often narrowly reserved for white, straight men and systematically denied to others, has been our messy national story. Slavery to abolition, Jim Crow to civil rights, codified patriarchy to women's suffrage, discrimination to legalized gay marriage, we inch along, bumper-to-bumper, down the highway of the moral universe.

We have, from time to time, coalesced to dull the sharper edges of capitalism: a graduated income tax, social security, unemployment benefits, Medicare and Medicaid, student loans and SNAP. And we have surfed waves of alternative community-based approaches to living, built on shared resources and distributed leadership.

But that sea has now flattened. And for a good fifty years, America has been dominated by unrepentant individual materialism. Unbridled capitalism, in cahoots with neo-liberalist government, has put its fat finger on the scale, tilting the balance between "we" and "I" so wickedly that, now, three people in the United States own more collective wealth than the bottom 50% combined. Of course, this grotesque inequity is the exact conundrum we set out to address in declaring our independence in the first place.

This tug of war between the common good and individual rights, often narrowly reserved for white, straight men and systematically denied to others, has been our messy national story.

From the captain's chair of my dusty vehicle, I reliably estimate that I can see a thousand cars of every conceivable color and size across this sprawling ten-lane superhighway. In front of me and behind, moving with me and against, there are tens of thousands more. Driving these sedans, pickup trucks, 18-wheelers and minivans are operators of every color and creed, race and religion, class and orientation – moving as if under the direction of Esther Williams.

The thruway is a poignant if banal portrait of a well-oiled social contract. We eschew certain rights to receive greater ones. With minor exception, we don't drive 120 miles per hour and, in turn, we have the luxury of a road to travel and a safe return home.

Road traffic serves as a rare alignment of self-interest and common good. We drive mindfully, only as fast as the car in front of us. We brake when needed and let people merge in, regardless of tint. The consequences of our autonomous actions are mutual. Recklessness results in a collective wreck. We may not share a destination but we do share a meritocratic destiny. Nobody gets downtown before anyone else.

Here, on the Interstate, the intersection of shared humanity and self-preservation, the common good and individual rights, is in perfect and ordinary lockstep. Our individual freedoms are dependent on each other.

In the end, there is both an irony and a beauty to the communal embrace of interdependence; a realization that our individual freedoms and the collective good are actually one and the same.

As I take the Topanga exit, I can't help but superimpose this metaphor on the coronavirus, which is again spiking dramatically across the United States with 50,000+ new daily cases. The solution to stanching the spread is, or was, hidden in plain sight. There is a playbook that other countries have successfully executed: mask-wearing, social distancing, identifying clusters, extensive testing and contact tracing, and quarantine of the infected. It works. And businesses can remain partially open. But this plan is predicated on social cohesion stemming from the willingness of an entire citizenry to put social good above perceived self-interest. In other words, you must get in your lane, put on some music, go slow, and take a breath. Eventually, you'll get there.

I can only imagine the patriotic pride felt among Kiwis, Taiwanese, Irish, Norwegians and Icelanders. Through shared sacrifice, they collectively stepped up to meet the greatest public health challenge of the millennia and conquered it, together. Yet in America - with our competing masks of patriotism - our greatest enemy has become each other. Our much-celebrated rugged individualism not only currently prevents us from entering Europe but many Americans cannot even travel to Connecticut.

In the end, there is both an irony and a beauty to the communal embrace of interdependence; a realization that our individual freedoms and the collective good are actually one and the same.

And perhaps our framers, despite their personal hypocrisies, were wise enough to comprehend this.

There is a spiritual lesson in this and it's not a novel one: The self is illusory. And this illusion, the notion that we are all distinct individuals living among other separate individuals in an external universe, is at the core of income inequality, racism, climate change, the unfettered spread of COVID and just about every other source of human misery.

Our ability to solve these existential riddles will stem from a collective spiritual revelation as much as political resolve.

I think about my Nana telling me stories in the car, fables of America and the promise of its dream. I glance at Micah wondering what stories am I going to tell her children's children?

Wishing all a Happy Interdependence Day.

WRITING EXERCISES

We've all been supported by our community or a specific someone. Reflect upon a time when you've been supported by the collective or another person, particularly when you perhaps could not have made it on your own. Write about what happened, how you felt, and how it felt to be supported by others.

Are there any areas in your life where you would be willing to sacrifice your self-interest for the common good? Describe them.

What are some potent examples of human interdependence?

WHO AM I?

We all have a story.

A dozen years ago, I co-founded Wanderlust, a company that produces large yoga festivals around the world. Our flagship event in Squaw Valley, California amassed enough yogis in leggings to swaddle the Taj Mahal in lycra. In the summer of 2012, I arrived on-site at our host hotel, the somewhat tattered Village-at-Squaw. Knackered from the trip, I was intent on quickly checking in to my usual ski condo and getting to our production meeting. As the stoner-cum-concierge bumbled through an unnecessary ream of clerical work, my patience began to fray. And I said it. It's the only time I have ever uttered this phrase and I shudder in the paternalism of it even as I type.

"Do you know who I am?" I said.

Befuddled, the desk clerk looked at me, turned to his counterpart and said, "This dude I'm checking in doesn't know who he is."

The fool speaks wisely as the wise man acts the fool.

Who am I? This is humanity's nagging question that chases us like a tail. It was famously asked by Ramana Maharshi in the eponymous tome on self-inquiry. Some never ask, suspended in their slumber. But once the shell is cracked, it becomes a life's pursuit. You remove sheath after sheath, like opening a set of Russian dolls, only to find yet another ontological riddle. I have dog-eared dozens of books trying to solve this conundrum from every available angle. But given the limited word count of this letter, I skip the lighter fare and ask:

Are we simply pure awareness perceiving transitory phenomena from moment to moment?

Or is our identity defined by the continuity of our life's experiences? Are we the summation of the stories that we tell ourselves about ourselves?

It was 1975 and I stood outside in the playground with the other kids. I was a kindergartner at the American School in Rio de Janeiro, Brazil.

The student body was mostly Brazilian with a smattering of foreign nationals from the United States, Britain and other parts of Europe. English was prominent in the classroom. But, on the playground, the linguistic currency was Portuguese, specifically Carioca, the slangy dialect native to Rio.

My absorbent brain sponged in the language with relative ease. We had moved to Rio from Santiago de Compostela, Spain. The transition from Galician Spanish to Portuguese is simpler for the non-conceptual child's temporal lobe. I was trading in sounds, language as music, not as vocabulary lessons. Of course, I was dragged into fluency by a force greater than anything cognitive; the innate instinct to belong.

The yard outside the main building was sloped at one end. And it was a favorite pastime to run along the flat section, then jump on to your bum and slide down the embankment. The grass had given way to dirt halfway down forming a landing strip of sorts. This was a ritual that I assiduously avoided. My body was not built for such nimble maneuvers. I was chubby. My paunch hung over my jeans. My thighs chafed just enough to wear down the denim between my legs to a thread-bare smoothness.

I parked myself on the sidelines listening to the school bully, Bobbito, direct traffic down the slope. The soundscape was chaotic. What possessed me I don't remember, but a sudden surge of confidence thrust me into line and I poised myself the best I could. My turn. I ran towards the slope, flinging myself awkwardly forward like a baby robin in first flight. It wasn't the smoothest landing and no distance records were set, but I did it. I made it down the hill. A couple barks of "Americano" my reward.

More sure of myself now, I trudged back up the hill and back into the queue. I cinched my belt a notch, tugged on my polo. This approach had more verve. I launched up, landed on my butt. And heard the sound. Curious how the brain can immediately process sonic phenomena into material reality. It was a ripping noise that made all other aspects of existence momentarily cease. I had torn my jeans straight down the crack of my ass. What's more, my tighty-whitey underwear, now available to the yard, had been stained by the dirt path.

This sent Bobbito into paroxysms of rapturous laughter as he belted out, "The American shat his pants." The infectious refrain was repeated again and again. "The American shat his pants. The American shat his pants." A catchy tune it must have been as it echoed across the yard. I stood at the bottom of the slope, nowhere to hide, eyes welled, lip bit, naked less my cloak of self-loathing and embarrassment.

Our own personal folklore can so often reinforce negative states of mind and keep us helplessly entangled in our emotional states. In many ways, living in the myths of our past and projecting them into the future keeps us bound to our pain and lost in thought. And it is our identification with this thought that can create the ego or a false sense of "I." In this way, our suffering is simply a fantasy of our own projection.

Fight, flight, freeze or, in this case, find the angle from which the least amount of people can see your stained underwear and shuffle back to the classrooms. Finally, off the Serengeti, and back into the relative safety of the admin building, I found my backpack and did my best to sling it cumbersomely behind me in attempt to camouflage my predicament. I limped into the nurse's office purporting an awful headache, one that apparently must have caused the nurse to think I shat my pants. "I must go home," I told her.

My mother was summoned and dutifully arrived. I made my brisk walk of shame back across the yard clumsily, as if I was in a three-legged race with myself. One last lingering coda of "The American shat his pants" faded into the distance.

This was the story of my youth, the hero's journey inverted, replete with all its classic shadow archetypes; the bully, the nurse, the tender mother, the ego, the shame, the self-loathing.

And this tale became the parable of my adulthood; the incessant need to be liked, to assimilate, to seek the approval of others, to base my identity in what other people think of me.

It's what led me to get into a taxi cab thirty-five years later with my daughters, recognize that the driver was Pakistani, and subconsciously muster a thick South Asian accent, "Greenwich Willage, pleece." My girls looking at me horrified. The cabby eyeballing my khakied whiteness with confusion and pity. I just wanted to connect.

It took me forty years to understand the difference between fitting in and belonging. Of course, I couldn't have expected my shit-stained 5-year old self to comprehend it, but Brené Brown finally articulated it perfectly. Fitting in is changing who you are in order to be accepted. Belonging is to be accepted while never compromising your authentic self.

I have compassion for that chubster. I was simply using the tools I had to survive. However, I now recognize that many of the seeds of my adult shortcomings were planted in this childhood yarn: the lack of self-love that pushed me down that slope in the first place, the false pride not to cry, the lying to the nurse, the shame born out of a lack of empathy for myself. These are all deficiencies of the ego.

Our own personal folklore can so often reinforce negative states of mind and keep us helplessly entangled in our emotional states. In many ways, living in the myths of our past and projecting them into the future keeps us bound to our pain and lost in thought. And it is our identification with this thought that can create the ego or a false sense of "I." In this way, our suffering is simply a fantasy of our own projection.

A layer pulls back. A doll cracks open to reveal another doll. And I try to move a step beyond.

Now that I look more critically at my story, as humorous as it may be to tell, I wonder if it's all bullshit. Maybe I slid down that slope and no one even cared? Maybe Bobbito was a voice inside my own head? To some extent, does it even matter? Whether fact or fiction, perhaps my ego sculpted this story to gird a false sense of identity?

And now I author questions because I am questioning my self-authorship, groping for truth in the dark.

Memory itself is a type of confirmation bias crafted by the psyche to reinforce one's current assumed identity? Are the stories we tell ourselves about ourselves simply the ego's attempt to retain sovereignty over an illusory self?

My playground story is among dozens of others that constitute the content of consciousness. And my personhood is certainly connected to the continuity of my life's experiences. I don't want to bypass trauma. Awful things can happen to people and that pain is real and must be processed.

However, as I sit in meditation, peeling back the koshas, I leave my satchel of stories, albeit briefly, at the door, if only to pick them up later. Just for an instant, there is a sensation of emptiness. For specks of time, the notion that "I" am somewhere inside my body as the thinker of my thoughts dissolves. I can only suppose this is what Eckhart Tolle means when he reduces "being" to the simple "I Am." I live nowhere near the enlightened state he inhabits, but I suppose to glimpse it is to know it exists.

In this wide, fleeting expanse, there is a simple conscious awareness of passing phenomena happening in this moment. And again now. In this quietness, there is truth. And truth has no story.

WRITING EXERCISES

Even the most evolved people struggle with writing about themselves. Yet, facing that fear can often help us find greater self-understanding.

Write down 4-5 words that your friends/family would use to describe you (good & bad).

_____

_____

_____

_____

Write down 4-5 words that you would use to describe yourself (good & bad).

_____

_____

_____

_____

Reflect on something you have done that epitomizes you in alignment with your best self.

_____

_____

_____

_____

_____

_____

_____

_____

_____

_____

_____

_____

_____

What is a quality about yourself that no one knows? Why do you keep this part of yourself hidden from the world?

_____
_____
_____
_____
_____
_____
_____

What are you most ashamed of? What are you most proud of?

_____
_____
_____
_____
_____
_____
_____
_____
_____
_____

What single quality might we all collectively manifest to bring about the greatest good in the world? What would the world look like if we could all embody this quality?

_____
_____
_____
_____
_____

_____

_____

_____

_____

_____

_____

_____

Write about a positive memory of yourself when you were younger.

_____

_____

_____

_____

_____

_____

_____

_____

_____

_____

Now describe a negative memory of yourself. Do these still relate to you as an adult?

_____

_____

_____

_____

_____

_____

_____

_____

_____

How do the qualities brought up by these memories align with you are now, and who you want to be?

_____

_____

_____

_____

_____

_____

_____

_____

_____

Who would you be without these memories?

_____

_____

_____

_____

_____

_____

_____

_____

_____

_____

_____

NAVIGATING POST-TRUTH

JULY 19

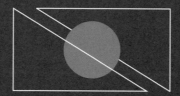

Tensions rose around the country as election primary results poured in, and states prepared for one of the most divisive and litigious election years in history, along with growing conflict over mail-in ballots. At least two Republican candidates came out as pro-QAnon, the conspiracy group that originated on the controversial 8chan image board and frequently promoted deep state conspiracies about an elite, primarily Democratic, "global cabal of Satan-worshipping pedophiles." Trust in both government and scientific institutions degraded as anti-mask protestors marched in Texas, a Georgia senator voided state face mask mandates, and Florida lawsuits argued that mask laws violate constitutional rights, while a growing number of Republican leaders began to finally recommend wearing them.

This inconsistent messaging from American leadership created more conflict as the President downplayed the effects of the virus, saying that 99% of cases were totally harmless and that the US had one of the lowest mortality rates in the world. Presidential aides and advisors sowed confusion by undercutting the country's lead infectious disease experts. Southern states began to bear the brunt of the coronavirus surge, as Florida became the epicenter with over 15,000 new cases reported in a single day. The pharmaceutical startup, Moderna, began a final phase of vaccine testing with 30,000 volunteers, just as the White House redirected all hospital COVID-19 data to an internal database, bypassing the CDC. Traumatized nurses returned home from NYC hospitals to Southern and Western states only to confront friends and family who believed the virus was a hoax.

On November 22, 1963, Arthur and Adeline sink into their divan to digest their chicken salad sandwiches. Per their post-lunch ritual, they flip on their guilty pleasure, As the World Turns. Just minutes into the program, the soap opera is interrupted by a news flash concerning an incident in Dallas, Texas with the Presidential motorcade. The episode continues only to be suspended again just minutes later.

Flanked by rotary phones and typewriters, Walter Cronkite appears in the CBS newsroom.[5] As he reports on the developing story, he is handed a memo. Cronkite removes his signature glasses and, in his inimitable tenor, announces the death of John F. Kennedy. For just a moment, Cronkite, visibly shaken, looks down and to the side, tightening his lips to hold the anguish of a nation. Lyndon Johnson will now become the 36th president of the United States. Adeline looks at Arthur and begins to cry. Arthur grips her hand reassuringly, "It's ok. We'll get through this."

This is how my grandparents and the rest of America got their news. Walter Cronkite, dubbed "the most trusted man in America," was the anchorman for the CBS Evening News for 19 years. It didn't much matter where you stood on the political spectrum, when Cronkite said it, it was accepted fact.

People of all ideological bents could bicker and debate their opinions, but diverging views were girded in a shared intersubjective understanding of truth. While certainly not infallible, the institution of journalism, with its code of ethics, independent fact-checking, multiple sources, and corrigendum engendered trust.

Hurtling through history alongside journalism, as if in a three-legged race towards progress, was science. Arthur credited technology for eradicating infectious disease, widespread famine and ending World War II. When I interviewed Adeline about how technology had impacted her life, she delivered an unexpected, if pre-feminist, answer. Evidently, the washer-dryer saved her twenty hours per week, which she used to volunteer at the local hospital. They were both starry-eyed with wonder as Apollo sent back images from the moon.

Science, like religion, provides us with a way to understand the world, where we come from and where we are going. However, science has proven more protean than other true world theories or Abrahamic traditions as it did not require blind fealty or incessant referrals back to old desert scrolls. Instead, it looked forward, humbly asking the question, "why?" And, not unlike journalism, it addressed its inquiries through a rigorous method of hypothesis, experimentation, observation, reasoning and determination.

Science and journalism, the way the world works and the medium through which we access that information, were the dual pillars of social cohesion for my grandparents' generation.

However, in 21st century America, this ceases to be true. We lie scattered, matches flung from a box.

Nowhere is this fracturing of society more apparent than in this pandemic. More than just a health crisis of epic proportions, COVID-19 in the United States is an epidemic of social polarization. The countries that have cohered around fairly straightforward solutions have stanched the viral spread, while those unable to unify are bickering their way into dystopia.

Certainly, this is partially due to illiberal leadership peddling "alternative facts," which slowly erodes the riverbanks of long-trusted institutions. Experts, despite years of study and research, are often pilloried as nothing more than effete, out-of-touch intellectuals.

But the erosion of a coherent narrative of unifying facts knitting our country together cannot simply be chalked up to deepening partisanship and the constant drone of "fake news." Medical science, for example, has sown its own seeds of mistrust, capitulating in many cases to big pharma. With misaligned incentives, pharmaceutical companies have biased studies and shrouded truth at human expense. Vioxx, a Merck drug developed for arthritis, caused 38,000 fatal heart attacks. OxyContin (Purdue Pharma) and other **prescription opioids** have killed 500,000 Americans. Proxy agricultural "science" has decimated our soil. There have been over 13,000 lawsuits filed against Monsanto in connection with its herbicide, glyphosate, which allegedly causes cancer.

Science, which once promised to deliver us from drudgery and the darkness of superstition, has so often been kidnapped by unfettered corporatism that it has squandered its moral credibility. That these very same companies - Bayer, Merck, P&G, GlaxoSmithKline and others – pump billions of marketing dollars into our media outlets elicits a well-founded skepticism about journalistic independence. Vioxx, in its time, was the most widely marketed pharmaceutical in history.

In the absence of trusted sources of fact, it becomes all too easy to fall prey to dystopic conspiracies of a New World Order. The decentralization of media distribution, which gives game show hosts and wellness influencers equal footing to news organizations as vectors for the proliferation of information, contributes to the unbridled spread of conspiracy theories – some that may be true, and many that lack any basis in fact.

If you espouse the notion that 5G is a means for spreading the coronavirus, you can find dozens of message boards and content to confirm your bias. In fact, you don't need to find them as those posts will simply find you through social media algorithms and artificial intelligence. Despite having no factual basis, activists that believe 5G is the agent for COVID have destroyed communication towers across Europe and even in Bolivia (where 5G doesn't even exist).

However, not all conspiracy theories are as specious or malicious as Pizzagate, Birtherism, and the denial of Sandy Hook. If I told you that a private prison company funded an organization comprised of legislators and private sector executives to write and pass legislation leading to mass incarceration, you might think I was wacko. But this is exactly what the Corrections Corporation of America and the American Legislative Exchange Council did.[6] Conspiracies are seductive because truth is often just as strange and twisted as fiction.

No political leaning has a monopoly on conspiracy. There is a bizarre emergent horse-shoeing of leftist conspiritualists and alt-right libertarians that is coming to a head around the potentially impending COVID vaccine, ratcheting up an already intense vaccination debate. This anti-vaxx alliance makes strange bedfellows of a slice of the "wellness" community, who sanctifies sovereignty over their bodies, civil liberties advocates who oppose governmental overreach, and "truthers" who fear that the illuminati will implant micro-chips as part of mass vaccination.

Last Friday, I had lunch with the nephew of John Kennedy, whose assassination could be seen as the grandfather of all conspiracies. Robert F. Kennedy Jr. has built a prolific career as an environmental litigator, winning hundreds of millions of dollars in class action suits against giant corporate polluters including DuPont and ExxonMobil. He recently prosecuted the California case against Monsanto for its use of the herbicide glyphosate. His record of representing indigenous and disadvantaged peoples is nothing less than sterling. His career has been defined by his rigorous application of science. Yet, he is an outspoken critic of mass vaccination, an issue that is currently so incendiary that intelligent debate is essentially nonextant.

To be clear, I support safe vaccination and clearly acknowledge the role immunization has played in eradicating small pox, taming other infectious diseases and even preventing cervical cancer. I sat across the table from Robert, a healthy dollop of skepticism on my polenta, for three hours. Robert possesses a charismatic and unparalleled fluency around vaccination, from case law and legislation to medical data and peer-reviewed science. He is of the few who ingests and comprehends primary source data. I challenge anyone to sit and listen to Robert's highly researched, if passionate, opinion and not believe that the notion of administering over 20 vaccines (the recommended schedule is itself contentious) to young children isn't at least worthy of some intelligent public discussion. But, currently, there is just all-caps screaming on Facebook.

With all of the countervailing forces at work, what is a citizen to do? What are we supposed to believe? How do we distinguish between ludicrous theories devised to divide and true corruption that warrants exposure? How do we find the social cohesion that is necessary not only to beat COVID but to address all of our salient global problems?

How much longer can we keep loving America and hating each other? Human success has always been predicated on our ability to cooperate flexibly at scale. Without social cohesion, we are chimps.

In my recent interview with Charles Eisenstein, he asked me, "Jeff, are you willing to be wrong for the sake of society?" I began to think about all the petty things in my own life that I have been wrong about. Schuyler told me a thousand times that taking Advil and Tums were bad for me. Stubbornly, I dismissed her until I learned that NSAIDs

Science, which once promised to deliver us from drudgery and the darkness of superstition, has so often been kidnapped by unfettered corporatism that it has squandered its moral credibility.

and antacids contribute to intestinal permeability, which was keeping me in a perpetual state of inflammation. I thought about the time I tried to drive my family to Vermont during hurricane Irene. Thankfully, Schuyler convinced me to stay in Connecticut as that storm veered west and devastated the Green Mountain state. I'll stop here because I could write a book about all the times Schuyler has been right. Maybe I will, after she's passed.

Indeed, the history of progress is the story of being wrong. The earth is flat. The sun orbits around it. Disease spreads through the bad air of rotting organic matter. Pythagoras, Galileo, Pasteur and indeed every ground-breaking scientist and philosopher challenged the paradigms of their time. And these affronts on the status quo are often quite unpopular. What progress across history does share, however, is critical thinking. And this may provide some flickering candlelight in the dark cave in which we find ourselves. The difference between thoughtful skepticism and fallacious conspiracy may be called wisdom.

As institutions wobble, individual citizens inherit a growing responsibility for the cohesion of society. Be inquisitive. Be humble. Think deeply and critically. Engage with and learn from others. Understand the best part of an opposing opinion. Apply methods of rigor in the quest for truth. Be willing to admit you are wrong.

Walter Cronkite isn't coming back.

WRITING EXERCISES

Humans often feel a need to be right. However, it has become harder to discern fact from fiction. Misinformation and deep fakes spread virally on social media clouding the truth. It is increasingly incumbent on individuals to practice both humility and critical thinking in the quest for truth.

Where do you get your facts?

What makes this source reliable in your opinion?

Can you think of a theory that society thought was correct, but turned out to be wrong?

How do you respond to others when you think they are wrong?

When you believe something, how much room do you leave for discovering new information about it?

Tell the story of a time you were wrong. How did you act in the aftermath?

How do you respond when you discover new information that feels very upsetting?

WALKING AMONG
THE DIVINE

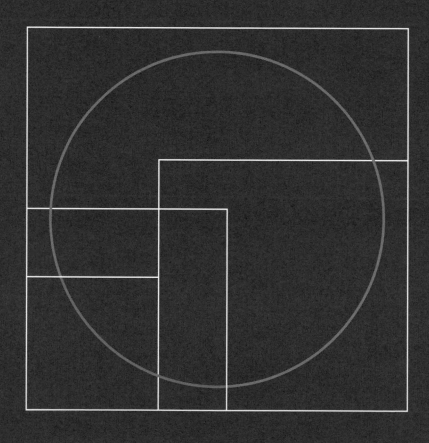

I am hiking the canyon loop, hunting ideas. I am edgy due to the constant ominous rustling in the brush along the path. Lizards darting, rabbits bounding, thrashers thrashing, rattlers slithering, imaginaries lurking. Nature welcomes home a long-lost cousin, wresting me from thought into the precarious present.

This experience, man wandering through the wood alone, senses sharpened, is old. For a moment, there is little that seems to separate me from the hominid forager ambling an East African savannah 70 millennia ago.

Except she walked among the divine, sharing her footpath with woodland gods and an occasional drunken satyr. Her tribe worshipped local deities that governed fire, rain, and the moon. Neighboring clans had their own provincial spirits. Moreover, she felt inextricably connected to her surroundings so much so that she shared a spiritual essence with the rock on which she stepped and the leaves that brushed her face.

With the decline of animism and the rise of Abrahamic traditions, God retired from earth. He moved to the putting green in the sky, slipped on a robe, grew a hipster beard, donned a Merlin's cap and absconded from the earthly plane.

This cleaving of the material and the mystical altered the way we understand and treat our worldly artifacts. We often perceive objects in the physical plane as devoid of divinity and, by extension, disposable.

Can you imagine the mystical wonder a Bic lighter might have inspired a million years ago as Homo Erectus sought to domesticate fire? In your mind's eye, envision the tribe huddled in awe around this neon yellow tube of plastic-encased butane, jabbing at its flint, agog as the flame springs forth. A gift from the Gods, it lies upon a hallowed shrine guarded assiduously by the bravest warriors. Now available in a 4-pack for 99 cents. Discarded mindlessly along with...

Plastic water bottles, party cups, straws, take-out containers, bottle caps, gift wrapping, coffee cups & lids, food packaging, plastic cutlery, outdated iPhones, antiquated stereo systems, drawers of chords and

Material objects can be sacred and embody the divine when they are unique and interrelated, when they hold a story.

adapters. All whirlpooling around a gyre in the Pacific Ocean twice the size of Texas. Out of sight, out of mind.

These artifacts of modernity are produced with the uniformity and efficiency that capitalism selects for. They signify almost nothing to us.

In many ways, our climate catastrophe is rooted in a self-authored story. In our quest to understand the nature of reality, give our lives meaning and establish structures of ethics, we concoct mythologies, the authorship of which we often attribute to the supernatural. The widespread acceptance of these myths become our inter-subjective understanding of the world and through them, humanity maintains a semblance of order.

Our Abrahamic scrolls gave humans dominion over nature and animals, useful authority for embarking on the agricultural revolution. This axiom is dubious not just because humans are quite literally animals of nature but also because it is at odds with our own experience of spirituality. Our epiphanies, our brief moments of divine connection, so often occur when we are re-immersed in nature.

But is there nothing sacred in the material? What about the hand-carved heart stone my daughter gave me to pack on long trips? Or my late grandfather's Naval dog tags? Or the heirloom locket that carries the bleached images of my immigrant story?

Think of the dress that your mother seamed and hemmed for you, how precious and irreplaceable it is. Consider the connectedness it holds. She made it especially for you with all its oddities and imperfections. When you wear it, or just look at it, she is in the room with you. Now consider the dress sewn in a Chinese sweatshop on the rack at Marshall's for $9.99 hung beside 100 frocks just like it. It's a standardized commodity made by someone completely anonymous. It elicits nothing.

Material objects can be sacred and embody the divine when they are unique and interrelated, when they hold a story.

Envision your sacred space, the place where you write, pray or meditate. It is not littered with plastic tchotchkes. Perhaps there is a photo there of your grandmother or a family treasure she gave you when you married or graduated. Maybe there are the mala beads you wore on your pilgrimage to Rishikesh. Or the novel you dog-eared when you hit rock bottom.

Better yet, visualize your ideal sanctum where you would be able to excavate and bare your soul. How much more deeply could you plumb the depths of your creative or spiritual self if you were to animate your surroundings with real value?

And what if we were to inspire the mundane? Can we alter our habits such that the contents of our closets and refrigerators more closely resemble the intention of our altar space?

Schuyler nearly fainted the other day when she waltzed into the kitchen to find me making my own oat milk. Admittedly, Phoebe had emptied the pre-packaged version and I was desperate for an iced coffee. But it really wasn't that difficult. And I savored that homemade iced latte as if I were sipping the sacramental wine from the Eucharist cup.

Often the only sacrifice we must make to feel a greater sense of connectedness is convenience. We are so concerned with losing time, that we misspend it.

Often the only sacrifice we must make to feel a greater sense of connectedness is convenience. We are so concerned with losing time, that we misspend it.

The circle of my hike is closing. And I laugh at myself. Nature is not rustling about me. I am the raucous interloper here, trudging heavy-footed through a forsaken habitat forgiving enough to still welcome me.

If we are to pursue spiritually rich, globally sustainable lives then we must dispense of the dualism that separates the realms of the sacred and the material. We must hand stitch them back together. We must eschew the disposable and value the unique, the necessary, and the objects that become the artifacts of our personal story. The entire physical world must become our altar space.

WRITING EXERCISES

We all have sacred objects in our lives, even if they don't live on an altar.

Survey your personal space and identify the objects in your life that hold divine meaning. Write their story: how they came to be in your life and why they are important to you.

What convenience would you sacrifice to feel a greater sense of connectedness?

A BEDTIME
FAIRY TALE
AUGUST 9

I am putting my daughter, Micah, to sleep and she asks me, "Daddy, if you could have one wish, what would it be?"

Considering tonight is my twenty-fifth wedding anniversary, I am inclined to tell her that my wish would be for her to put herself to sleep, but that seems cruel, so I demur. If there is one parental pastime that I dread and will miss in profound and equal measure, it is this ritual. It tests both psychological endurance and physical dexterity. I summon and spin the same thread-bare yarns of childhood, listening attentively for the parasympathetic breath of slumber. Not yet free, I plot my exodus, furtively sidling toward the edge of the bed. Like a parole officer sensing illicit activity, Micah rolls over and imprisons my mid-section with her flopping and now lifeless arm.

"I'm not asleep yet. Tell me the story of when you met mommy."

It's 1988. Long-haired and rumpled in my favorite flannel, I sat in the back row of freshman art class. If it had been possible, I would have opted for a desk on the scaffolding outside the window, anything to avoid the icy gaze of the persnickety art history teacher. Miss DePoint was preternaturally tall, always in a well-fitted skirt suit, her tight grey bob accentuating her angular chin. She wielded a yardstick that she used as a pointer and, at any moment, she could have pivoted toward me, Jadis-like, endlessly long, and turned me to stone. She flashed Bernini on the overhead projector and tapped at the screen rhythmically with her lengthy wand.

With clockwork precision, Schuyler, still in her talc-y leotard, sauntered into class five minutes late and folded her sinewy frame into the seat diagonal from me. Completely unfazed by Miss DePoint's displeasure, she fetched a grapefruit from her dance bag, clawed both hands into its top and ripped back the peel. This vigorous action unbottled an aerosol of grapefruit particulates that, like fairy dust, infused the back of the room. As the citrus cloud enveloped me, I fell under a mystical spell.

And, in a moment, we were sculpture. Hovering above her, I thrust my golden arrow into her heart. She, with her head thrown back, lay in a

Commitment is often misconstrued as limitation and framed within the parentheses of sacrifice, of what one must give up. However, the bedrock of our unconditional mutual pledge has allowed us to take madcap risks and chase uncertain dreams, knowing, that in failure, there is the comfort of allegiance to break our fall. In this way, we have known commitment only as freedom.

state of transcendent bliss. The ecstasy of Saint Teresa. This was the epiphany that shuttered my faithless childhood and launched my devotion to Schuyler.

My chivalrous pursuit of this maiden knew no bounds. I boarded my trusty 4-wheeled steed and stalked my quarry stealthily from city block to city block. I learned to speak with my hands, like her. I rambled barefoot on the perilous terrain of upper Manhattan, slaying the dragons of my motherless adolescence. Until one night, intertwined, we collapsed right on the sidewalk of Amsterdam Avenue and lay there for hours, baring full witness to our eternal embrace.

"You still awake, Micah?"

"Daddy, tell me the part where you and mom get old."

"Well, we're not exactly old yet, but..."

See-sawing between lover and beloved, we romped across campgrounds and far-flung hostels, slept in hammocks and in the hallways of train cars. We learned foreign tongues and stole across borders. We owned little and wanted for nothing.

As adulthood knocked, I climbed beanstalks of steel and glass and spun straw to gold with both ardor and folly. Schuyler stepped onto stages, to act out the plays of others and play out the acts of self. We toiled, built studios, launched festivals, forged friendships and scrawled books. We raised the chalice in victory and we suffered epic defeats at the hands of neighboring kingdoms.

The human story is the accrual of hundreds of these triumphs and just as many failures that slowly, against our will, beget wisdom.

Commitment is often misconstrued as limitation and framed within the parentheses of sacrifice, of what one must give up. However, the bedrock of our unconditional mutual pledge has allowed us to take madcap risks and chase uncertain dreams, knowing, that in failure, there is the comfort of allegiance to break our fall. In this way, we have known commitment only as freedom.

And then we had three little bears with goldy locks. (My mighty rapier valiantly delivered three consecutive X chromosomes, if only to avoid a duel over circumcision.) And, with three princesses, we were summarily dethroned, usurped from the center of our own universe. No longer the nucleus, we became electrons looking in on life, not out at it.

Self-obsession dissolves when you would die, without a moment's hesitation, for someone else. And this phenomenon of parenthood transforms the geometry of love from a linear affair between partners, to a multi-dimensional shared consecration of your children.

Young, unruly chaotic lust gives way to care, respect and also distinctly unmagical transaction. No longer is our love the rapturous, intertwined passion of teenagers on a city sidewalk. We're more linked paper clips than a double helix, free to go our separate ways until the curved edges of our union pull us back in line. It's an officious type of middle-aged tenderness. I love you. Pass the hole puncher.

Who will drive the carriage to procure provisions? Who will deliver the girls unto seminary or to the athletic pitch? Who will pay the state tariffs and manage the gold? But the fairy tale need not completely become the laundry list.

Over time, devoted partners fulfill each other's needs. In the absence of need, a profound sort of love springs forth. Love, in this way, is not an emotion that visits the castle as a party guest only to leave before the strike of midnight. In wholeness, one becomes the source of love, not the subject that perceives it as transitory sensation.

Your mother and I were two young saplings planted too close together. We are often now indistinguishable from each other, not just because our gnarled tree trunks have fused, but because our love, as essence, impervious to the vacillations of space and time, is not separable.

On my best days, I still feel like in a painting. Dreamy, not altogether of this place. I want to tear her away from this dull care. And walk and talk and do nothing and leave nothing undone.

"Can you go to sleep now, sweetheart?"

"Ok. Daddy, but just answer me. If you could have one wish, what would it be?"

I ponder. She can sense I have an answer now. Could it be a trip to Disneyland? Or a Pomeranian? Perhaps a new trampoline?

"Micah, I wish your mother and I, a long time from now, will die on the same day."

I feel guilty giving her this macabre answer. But what her mind cannot grasp, her heart understands easily. She gives me a hug. I forget that she is closer to God than I am.

"Good night brave sir Micah. I love you."

"I love you, too."

To what or to whom are you committed?

_____
_____
_____
_____
_____
_____
_____
_____
_____
_____

How does that commitment make you feel?

_____
_____
_____
_____
_____
_____
_____
_____
_____

In what ways is this commitment liberating and in what ways does it feel limiting?

Are you ready to commit yourself to something new? If so, what is it?

THE OTHER EPIDEMIC

AUGUST 16

By August 2020, unemployment benefits for many states were cut in half as eviction bans lifted. Deaths were again on the rise, despite shrinking case numbers—a fallout from the summer surge in the South. There was a recorded increase in substance abuse, anxiety, depression and suicidal thoughts for young adults, Black and Latino people. Early in the pandemic, former California Health Director Dr. Sonia Angell expressed concern over the disparity in COVID-19 related deaths, especially among Black and Latino people. In Florida, Black people were dying at a rate double that of white people, and the death rate was almost three times as high among younger adults. Many of the younger victims had diabetes, asthma or were obese, showing that those with health problems faced higher risk regardless of age. Economically disadvantaged people, along with many ethnic minorities, worked essential jobs, lived off of smaller budgets and often had less access to healthy food and lifestyles. Many were unable to pay their rent and continued to rely on food banks for supplies. Over 100 million Americans have diabetes or prediabetes, and 122 million have cardiovascular disease. Hypertension and diabetes are two of the most common comorbidities associated with dying from COVID-19.

Meanwhile, streaming services like Disney+, Hulu, and ESPN+ experienced high growth, with over 100 million subscribers, as people quarantined at home. Revenue from digital gaming went up more than 50% since April, increasing from 20 billion in 2010 to 160 billion in 2020.

We're late for soccer. It's always the elusive shin guards, hunkered away in some shadowy corner. I suppose I, too, might sequester at the prospect of the flailing cleats and errant kicks of 10-year old girls.

Lolli sanctifies punctuality, an odd proclivity for a girl her age. Any remote intimation of tardiness plugs the chatterbox, that normally lives inside her head, into a speaker and an endless stream of anxious inner dialogue is amplified out into the world. I wonder where she gets this loquacity.

I am channeling all my parental empathy to pull back from DEFCON 5. Lolli is fiddling with the AYSO app, checking the game schedule for the tenth time, when she discovers that I am the parent responsible for bringing this week's snack. F*cking snack. Obviously, I have not procured the cursed snack.

This post-game pastime is often more sacred than the game itself. Somehow, when a parent provides a superlative snack, there is a mystical halo effect that gilds the child a profound sense of belonging and confidence.

The beleaguered designated parent, saddled with bulging satchels of mystery grub, are eyed with the scrutiny of a military aid carrying the nuclear football. Hushed whispers weave their web, "What's the snack going to be today?"

Any consternation about potential lateness is now usurped by the absence of snack. Lolli's countenance matches the color of her crimson jersey. She's apoplectic.

The moment has arrived for me to activate my rarely invoked Zen master super powers. I drop Lolli at the pitch and assess the situation. Can I acquire a satisfactory snack and return in time for my part of the sporting ritual, the nervous pacing of the sidelines punctuated by the occasional bark of encouragement?

Lolli's games are at Johnnie Cochran Middle School just off Crenshaw

Boulevard in Mid City, Los Angeles. The non-descript appellation, Mid City, is appropriate in exactly the way you might imagine; an endless straggle of asphalt in every direction, pocked by bi-level mini-malls and fast-food fare from Arby's to El Pollo Loco. Google Maps tells me there are no less than a dozen 7-Elevens within the throw of a stone. In the hopes of finding something with a semblance of nutritional value, I am looking, in vain, for a grocery story. I just start driving.

Finally, nestled between a 99-cent store and a laundromat, I spot a pile-up of grocery carts in front of a concrete fortress, the contents of which is only drearily revealed by a lime-green neon sign spelling ARKET, the "M" having met an untimely death. I park, hustle in and survey the savannah for options. There is an aisle completely dedicated to soda and sport drink of every fluorescent hue. Another reserved for savory chips of all geometries. And yet another preserved almost exclusively for variations of Oreos. There are also ketchups and sauces, spreads and breads.

If you were to pick up any single one of these items and read the label, they would share one common ingredient: refined sugar. In fact, added sugar is in over 80% of the foods on the grocery store shelf. And, in food deserts like this one, the percentage is even higher.

This missive is not a dissertation on sugar, the food industry or obesity. I couldn't possibly address the depth of this scourge on society within the parameters of this article. If you want thorough, researched information about the public health and socio-political implications of processed food and refined sugar then read or listen to Dr. Robert Lustig or Dr. Mark Hyman. Still, here are some broad points.

The consumption of sugar and sugary sweeteners, mostly in the form of high-fructose corn syrup (HFCS), has skyrocketed over the past 100 years. In 1915, the average annual sugar consumption per person was 17.5 pounds. As of 2011, the number rose to 150 pounds of sugar per person annually.[7]

The average American now consumes 30 teaspoons (or 120 grams) of sugar per day. That is approximately double the US government recommendation. A significant portion of this supplemental sugar is delivered in beverage form. Perhaps unsurprisingly, a 12 oz. can of Mountain Dew contains 46.5 grams of sugar. More startling though is the prevalence of sugar in beverages that are marketed as part of a healthy lifestyle like sport "hydration" drinks. Or consider a 20 oz. bottle of Sobe Energize Green Tea, an innocuous, even purportedly "enlightened," thirst quencher, which packs a whopping 61 grams.

Table sugar (sucrose) is a disaccharide compromised of glucose and fructose which, in digestion, are separated and metabolized very differently. Glucose provides calories for cells. The liver turns excess fructose into fat. Fructose is known to induce leptin resistance and greatly increase the risk of developing obesity. As leptin plays an important role in regulating hunger, suppressing leptin release can produce an insatiable appetite and lead to over-consumption.

Why is high-fructose corn syrup so omnipresent? It's cheap, about half the price of cane sugar, largely because the Big Food industry and corn refiners having successfully lobbied for subsidies that are guaranteed through the Farm Bill. The production of high-fructose corn syrup (and other sweeteners) under their true cost of production is a citizen-funded, government-enabled grant to companies like Coca-Cola who pack their drinks with sodium to make you thirstier and mask it with cheap HFCS. This allows Big Beverage to market its product in increasingly larger portion size. We have all witnessed, and perhaps experienced, the 44 oz. Big Gulp, the daily consumption of which will yield fifty-seven pounds of fat by year's end.

What is the by-product of ubiquitous high fructose corn syrup (and processed food in general)? From 2000 through 2018, the prevalence of obesity in the United States increased from 30.5% to 42.4%. What is obese? Obesity in adults is defined as a body mass index (BMI) of greater than or equal to 30. BMI is calculated as weight in kilograms divided by height in meters squared, rounded to one decimal place. To save you some math, a BMI of 30 for someone 6 feet tall is 222 pounds. A BMI of 40 (severely obese) is 295 pounds. And the prevalence of severe obesity has increased in the last 20 years from 4.7% to 9.2%. For comparison, obesity rates in China hover around 6%. Little doubt remains that there is a correlation between sugar consumption and obesity rates. BMI is not always a reliable metric on an individual level as it does not account for greater muscle mass, bone density and overall body composition. However, it is generally accepted as a large-scale statistical measurement.

Sugar is also known to suppress the immune system.[8] Just consuming 100 grams of sugar can suppress white blood cell function by 40% for at least 5 hours.

Why interrupt your Sunday brunch with this disquisition on the evils of sugar at this very moment? Because while COVID-19 is a nasty, highly transmissible and potentially fatal virus, lurking behind the pandemic, is a more pervasive and insidious epidemic. We consume too much sugar. We are increasingly obese and living with chronic disease and inflammation. In our immune compromised state, we increase our susceptibility to viruses.

Escalating obesity prevalence is directly tied to sky-rocketing rates of chronic disease, most notably diabetes. There are 35 million American adults (10.5% of the population) with Type 1 diabetes and nearly 100 million additional people that are pre-diabetic. The estimated domestic total economic cost of diagnosed diabetes in 2017 was $327 billion.[9]

There is a distinct socio-economic component to these data that often correspond with racial inequities.[10] Black men are 7% more likely to be obese than white men. And Black women are the most disproportionately impacted group with obesity rates at 57% (17 points higher than white women). Comorbidities, the simultaneous presence of two chronic diseases or conditions in a patient, such as obesity and diabetes have contributed to a COVID-19 age-adjusted fatality rate among Black Americans that is 3.7 times White Americans.[11]

I cast no aspersions on people carrying extra weight. My childhood chubbiness and its accompanying self-esteem issues have been thoroughly documented in my prior screeds. And, in full candor, I am currently in a knife fight with a pair of muffin tops that are cresting over my belt loops as I approach 50. To be clear, being healthy should not be confused with the commodification of wellness which projects unattainable images of perfection in an attempt to create a feeling of deficiency and then markets products and services to address that perceived lack. Being well is not about appearance. It's about health and, thus, should not be judged.

The media floods us with daily stratagems to address the riddle of snowballing COVID diagnoses. Indeed, there was a point when America could have followed the lead of other nations and quashed the spread through well-documented policies that include a combination of personal responsibility and governmental leadership. These tactics include mask-wearing, social distancing and personal hygiene in combination with mass testing, contact tracing and the curbing of superspreading events. (By most estimates, just 10 to 20 percent of coronavirus infections account for 80 percent of transmissions.[12]) Incompetent leadership may have ironically informed a new strategy for international terrorism. "Leave the United States alone. They'll do themselves in."

While there is a glut of newscasters, scientists and CDC officials hammering home important, if conventional, policies, there is a deafening silence from the media and the mainstream medical community around personal health, the pre-COVID-19 ground conditions in America that have led to such widespread transmissions and fatalities (5.2MM cases and 166,000 deaths at publishing[13]).

There is data emerging suggesting a correlation between excess weight and COVID-19 severity.

A recent OpenSAFELY study reports the risk of dying from COVID-19 increased by 27% among obese individuals and was doubled in patients with a body mass index greater than 40.[14]

In a prospective cohort study of patients with COVID-19 from New York City, the prevalence of diabetes and obesity was higher in individuals admitted to hospitals than those not admitted to hospitals (34.7% vs 9.7% for diabetes and 39.5% vs 30.8% for obesity, respectively).[15]

Instead of celebrating the elixir of binges, from Chubby Hubby to Netflix, that has conspired to coin the term "the COVID fifteen" (referring to weight gain from inactivity during quarantine), we could be seizing this moment to have an initiative for public health:

- To promote exercise, mindfulness practices and proper nutrition as a means to build healthy immunity.

- To take on Big Food and hold them accountable by, at the very least, internalizing their true costs.[16]

- To educate widely on nutrition, promote cooking and community gardens.

- To provide incentives for grocery stores to enter underserved neighborhoods and stock fruits and vegetables.

- To make SNAP benefits redeemable online such that these services can deliver to underserved communities.

- To consider taxes on egregious products (similar to cigarette tax).

- To enlarge the FVRx program (fruit and vegetable prescription program for children).[17]

- Pass a new Farm Bill.[18]

There is very little public discourse focused on what we need to do to improve the underlying well-being of society. And while robust immune systems are not going to protect us from more lethal viruses (like Ebola), there is plenty of good reason to address the underlying roots causes of our societal dis-ease. We can leverage this moment to invest in our communal health or continue lining the pockets of Big Pharma to incessantly treat the mal-effects.

Further, well-being must cease to be a class privilege. Running, walking, practicing yoga, core exercise and meditating require time – and the priceless commodity of discipline - but virtually no financial resources.

The access both logistically and financially to high quality food, however, must be addressed.

Enough confabulating, I am late for kick-off. I return to the game sheepishly with my bags of treats. Fifteen individually packaged bags of chips, a case of juice boxes, a pack of Chips Ahoy and a watermelon that I manage to carve up with an old library card.

The Red Devils are crushed 8-1, mostly due to the opposition's pair of dazzling Brazilian twins. The mourning quickly dissipates though as snack is unveiled. Lolli, who knows my sugar rant too well, is relieved by my selections. She gives me a nod as if to acknowledge and assuage the wave of hypocritical guilt she knows I am surfing. The team drowns their sorrows in corn syrup. Finally, out of pure sympathy, a compassionate mom reaches for a jagged slice of watermelon. We look at each other, then together at the kids and simultaneously shrug in resignation.

WRITING EXERCISES

We all have bad habits. Sometimes, these habits become addictions that undermine our well-being. Society doesn't make it easy for us to manage our habits and keep them in moderation. As noted in the article, sugar is added to almost everything. Alcohol can be bought on virtually every street corner and its consumption is celebrated at almost any event.

What is your relationship to food, specifically sugar?

Are you aware of the ill-effects of your addictive behaviors? Where do they show up?

What are some ways that you can enhance your well-being in the year ahead?

FROM STRAW TO STEEL

AUGUST 23

I am facing the daunting task of setting up three daughters for successful distance learning. I keep reminding myself there is no playbook for parenting during a pandemic. This helps assuage the guilt I feel for engaging in petty acts of bribery. We have resorted to cajoling our kids into engaging with Zoom lessons for interminable hours by adopting a range of lovable furry animals. This inducement elicited a fierce backseat debate between my two youngest.

"Lolli, what do you want, a cat or a dog?" asked Micah.

"I think cats are cuddlier, so I'd say a cat," replied Lolli.

"You're such a dog hater!" retorted Micah.

From the driver's seat, I couldn't help but interject and point out to Micah that she had just used a straw man argument against Lolli. Neither saw the relevance of The Wizard of Oz in their dispute.

Straw man arguments riddle the invective of social media. Here's one I just picked off Facebook.

Poster 1: I believe that building a wall on the border will stem the tide of illegal immigration.

Poster 2: Only a racist would post that.

In this example, regardless of what one may think about the efficacy or ethics of a border wall, Poster 2 "stood up a straw man."

A straw man is a form of argument that creates the impression of refuting an opinion. However, the real underlying idea of the opinion under discussion is not addressed or properly negated. One who engages in this fallacy is said to be "attacking a straw man" because it's distinctly unchallenging to knock down a man of such flimsy substance.

The typical straw man argument creates the illusion of having completely defeated an opponent's proposition through the covert replacement of it with a different proposition and the subsequent refutation of that false argument ("to knock down a straw man") instead of the opponent's true and original proposition.

There has been a population explosion of straw men on social media. The modern iteration of the public square is the perfect breeding ground for emotional and reductionist debates about highly charged and nuanced subjects. Crouched behind the safe anonymity of their screens, people circumvent substantial debate about ideas and condemn the people who hold them. This is referred to as an ad hominem attack (as exemplified above) and fuels our hyper-polarized and balkanized society.

I want to propose an alternative approach for public debate: Steelmanning

No, it's not a series of high-intensity workout videos. It's actually a debate technique I have adopted that has emerged directly out of penning this weekly missive.

As a general note, I make my absolute best efforts to tackle thorny topics respectfully, thoughtfully, and with research that conforms to a journalistic code of ethics. My goal is to stimulate complex, long-wave conversations that transcend the parameters of social media's tight goal posts. However, I freely admit to making plenty of mistakes and that there are people who not only possess opposing viewpoints, but also have profound expertise on particular topics I do not. I hear from them. And I have become very grateful for their thorough and scrupulous criticism because that is how I learn and grow.

Steelmanning could be considered the opposite of strawmanning.

> Here is how it works:
>
> · Identify an opinion you have on a particular issue.
>
> · Identify an opinion you have on a particular issue.
>
> · Find someone who disagrees with your position.
>
> · Humbly listen to her opinion, while discarding your own pre-existing bias (to the degree that it is possible).

- Fully ingest and process her argument.

- Attempt to re-express her position clearly, vividly, and fairly out loud to her.

- Enumerate any points of agreement (especially if they are not matters of general or widespread agreement).

Some additional texture: Before jumping into this exercise, commit to a thorough, thoughtful inventory that girds your original position. Gather facts and data from reliable, ethical sources to support your opinion. Ideally, find a partner who is thoughtful and shares the spirit of this joint exercise. When listening, do so without facially expressing dismay or disgust. Note what information triggers you and note where you are most intrigued. In the re-expression of her position, focus on the best and most compelling parts of her argument.

And if winning an argument is really what drives you, steelmanning is perhaps the sharpest of weapons, since you hone your own argument by thoroughly understanding the most convincing elements of the opposing view.

This technique also works in reverse where your partner will steel man you. This exercise is done preferably in person or on Zoom as visual interaction is usually less dehumanizing. You may choose to record it so you can re-experience it and also model it for others. If you can't find a willing opponent, you can practice with someone by simply assuming opposing roles.

This drill yields myriad results. It produces more fortified opinions. It creates the possibility for common ground by humanizing your rival. Through the free exchange of ideas, novel and more evolved positions may cream to the top. It rounds the edges of our codified and binary ideological boxes. Sam Harris and Jordan Peterson in debate provide an excellent example of this technique.[19]

Steelmanning, however, is more than a nifty debate technique. It is a potent personal development tool.

It develops humility and tolerance by forcing you to assume that the people with whom you disagree, as much as you might dislike them and

The enemy is the idea, not the person. And we should focus on eradicating flawed ideas, not dehumanizing those who hold them.

their ideas, still have something to teach you. It fosters empathy and compassion, counteracting our impulse to quickly dismiss or declare victory. It broadens our minds by pushing the limits of what we might consider possible. It develops humility and our ability to listen. It roots us in logic and rationality by underscoring the notion that we are debating ideas, not debasing people. The enemy is the idea, not the person. And we should focus on eradicating flawed ideas, not dehumanizing those who hold them.

A healthy liberal democracy requires public discourse and, by extension, a proper forum to have it. The theory of the "marketplace of ideas," stemming from the writings of John Stuart Mill and John Milton, posits that the free dissemination of ideas creates a social process in which truth competes and eventually wins out over falsehood. Of course, these great minds were philosophizing before social media, which I have exhaustively prosecuted as an abysmal sandbox for thoughtful debate. Twitter, Facebook, and Instagram (and their virtual offspring) are permanent fixtures in our public house. If we can't learn to check our trigger fingers and, when possible, migrate our arguments off of these platforms and challenge each other to engage in more humanizing environs, we are going to burn the house down.

A steelman rides into battle brandishing not a torch but an olive branch, a commitment to his or her own opinions tempered by a sincere openness to learn and grow. If we believe in liberal democracy, and there's every reason to consider it the best system of social organization, then let us steel our convictions through this humble practice.

WRITING EXERCISES

Engage in the process of steelmanning through writing and then experiment with it with a willing partner.

Find a thoughtful, well-researched source that posits an opinion that diverges from your own. Absorb this contrary belief and then write it down as if it were your own, drawing on the most compelling components of it.

Experiment with three or four different issues. Note how your original opinion changes, moderates and fortifies.

A BRIDGE TO AMERICA'S FUTURE

AUGUST 21

In 1898, Nathan Kiva, a nineteen-year old boy from Odessa, left his shtetl and embarked on the harrowing voyage across the Atlantic. Two months later, tempest-tost, his ship pulled into New York harbor, America's golden door. Upon arriving at Ellis Island, he queued up and, finally, the immigration official asked for his surname.

"Kiva," he replied.

The administrator wrinkled his face, "Vocation?"

"Ich bin ein gluzman," Nathan mustered in Yiddish-inflected German.

"Ok, Nathan Glassman. Move along."

Move along he did, out of the shadow of liberty's torch and to Chicago. He purchased a small pushcart that he wheeled through the city repairing glass. Two years later, he met a Romanian woman, Dora, at the local temple. They soon married and, in 1918, my grandmother, Adeline Glassman, was born.

In 1942, Adeline gave birth to her only child, Richard Krasno, my father. In 1958, Richard met his high school sweetheart at Evanston Township High School. Jean Cullander's grandparents had immigrated from Scotland and Sweden. Jean's mother, Fran, played the bells in her church group. She was part of the same United Methodist congregation for 92 years until she moved to Connecticut.

Richard and Jean fell in love and, mollifying all parties by accommodating none, they consecrated their vows at the Unitarian Church, a Christian theology that maintains that Jesus was inspired by God in his moral teachings but he was not God incarnate.

In 1970, Jeffrey Patrick Krasno was forceps-extracted at Lying Inn Hospital at the University of Chicago. The name Jeffrey is derived from a Middle French variant for Gottfried. Patrick, initially rooted in Latin, is a popular Irish name and was one of my father's best friends. Krasno is Russian meaning "red" or "beautiful." I opt for the latter.

By the time I was seven, I had moved 10 times across Europe and Brazil. My olive skin, shades darker than that of my parents and brother, carries intimations of a promiscuous mailman. This jumble of genetics, faiths and peripatetics has always made self-identification a confounding process for me.

I am a Scottish-Romanian-Swedish, Jewish-Methodist-Unitarian dude with a French, Irish, and Russian name who speaks a number of languages and doesn't look like his parents. In lingua canis, you might call me a mutt, just lovable enough. In terms of nationality, all of these far-flung traits and ethnicities makes me distinctly American.

What if our fundamental understanding of "spiritual" truths like equality, empathy, love and compassion was not Judeo-Christian (or based in any religious doctrine), but, instead, essentially human? Or perhaps intrinsically American, in its highest incarnation?

My family was part of a major inflow of immigrants in the late 19th and early 20th centuries, primarily from Eastern and Southern Europe. My story, though, is hardly exceptional. In fact, unless you are descended from Native Americans or from people brought to America against their will, then you share my immigrant story in some fashion.

Two Tuesdays ago, around 1pm PDT, my phone erupted with text messages. Joe Biden, the Democratic nominee for president, had officially selected California senator Kamala Harris as his running mate, a significant milestone given she is the first Black woman and the first of South Asian descent in American history to be on a major party's presidential ticket.

It is not my intention to legislate Harris' political credentials here. I will simply state that, in my opinion, she is eminently qualified to be either president or vice-president. She is experienced, "tough" (as if that adjective would ever be used to describe a male candidate), articulate and progressive. And, like my beloved Nana, she is also reported to make a mean tuna salad.

Harris' selection underscores the rise of a new wave of children of immigrants, or second-generation Americans, as a growing political and cultural force. Her parents, Shyamala Gopalan and Donald Harris, both immigrated to the United States, from India and Jamaica respectively, to receive doctorate degrees at the University of California, Berkeley. They were part of a mid-century influx of immigration from Asia, Latin America and the Caribbean.

Harris also grew up in a multi-faith household that accommodated both Christianity and Hinduism. As an adult, she married Doug Emhoff, a Brooklyn-born Jewish lawyer. She currently identifies as Baptist.

In a time of shifting racial demographics and religious pluralism and disaffiliation, Harris' candidacy represents a political and cultural bridge to the future of America, one that significantly diverges from the white Christian majority of the past.

Nationwide, for the first time in American history, whites make up less than half of the population under the age of 16, a trend that is driven by larger numbers of Asians, Hispanics and people who are multiracial.[20] Interracial marriage rates are especially high for second-generation Hispanics (26%) and among Asians (23%). Today, more than a quarter of American adults are foreign-born immigrants (approximately 42 million) or the American-born children of immigrants (about 25 million).

Here's a snapshot at what the future demographic composition of America resembles: In 2042, whites will no longer be a majority in America. And, at the current growth rate, a majority of Americans will identify as religiously disaffiliated by 2050. Whether one views this inexorable reality as deeply hopeful or profoundly threatening is among the greatest wedge issues of this moment.

What does this multi-racial, progressively more secular future mean in terms of how we self-identify and where we anchor morality and ethics?

Humans have invented myriad ways to understand the world and find purpose. Abrahamic religions, as heuristics, are useful in so far that they provide community, identity and moral values. However, the modern utility of texts that support the idea of fatally stoning someone for apostasy, homosexuality, talking back to your parents or not being a virgin on your wedding day is deeply questionable. Nor is the promise of paradise in the form of 72 virgins for martyrs carrying out the most extreme actions of the jihad ethically acceptable. In the end, despite any veneer of tolerance, these religions all ultimately claim the last word of God and are fundamentalist in this way. Sure, worship whomever you want, but you'll be going to a hot place for eternity. Increasingly, young people simply do not resonate with this dogmatism.

Still, however, because we see many of the same universal truths posited in all religions and, also, because people of every faith have all claimed spiritual epiphanies experienced within the context of their own faith, this consilience suggests that there is some moral and ethical structure that occurs prior to the existence of religion. There is a basic and universal human intuition that recognizes compassion, love, empathy, charity and forgiveness as perennial virtues.

As we hurtle into a post-religious society, cohering around a reliable moral and ethical structure that does not devolve into relativism will be a formidable, if exhilarating, challenge. In the absence of religion (or, at least, one dominant faith), the future of how we differentiate between proper and improper decisions and actions may emerge from community, from how we co-exist and thrive together. And, in the United States, the way we live together will be increasingly secular and multi-racial.

What if our fundamental understanding of "spiritual" truths like equality, empathy, love and compassion was not Judeo-Christian (or based in any religious doctrine), but, instead, essentially human? Or perhaps intrinsically American, in its highest incarnation?

Identifying on the basis of race or religion can inform a sense of self, proudly connect us to a culture and a community, but, even in its best effect, it more often separates us. As the melting pot simmers and churns and institutional religion declines, race and faith will become less determinant in how we self-identify. This is where community and, by extension, nationhood, may become more important and central in the establishment of our identity and moral structures.

In trying to envision the future, messages in bottles can often provide clues. 70 millennia ago, homo sapiens experienced a near-extinction level event. It is posited that the Toba volcano super-erupted in Indonesia spewing forth tons of ash, creating a cooling effect on an already cold earth. There is evidence that the average temperature dropped 20-plus degrees in some locations and the great grassy plains of Africa significantly receded. This disaster decimated the human population as hominids retreated back to East Africa. It is speculated that the human population was reduced to a couple thousand bedraggled foragers.

Expanding the marketplace of ideas and ethics to equally include a variety of cultures, races and traditions should yield, from a purely evolutionary perspective, better philosophies and stronger social cohesion versus a society that requires assimilation into one dominant culture.

In his brilliant book Tribe, Sebastian Junger describes the propensity of humans to profoundly bond together in disastrous times. Few instances could have been more devastating than the Toba eruption. From the brink of extinction, humans forged cooperative systems, found common ethical frameworks and slowly repopulated over ten thousand years. This period in history could be considered pre-racial and pre-religious (though undoubtedly there were local deities).

The human population dwindled to such an extent that it created a genetic bottleneck, a drastic narrowing of diversity, that extends into the present-day. Though we often focus on what divides us, genetically, we are all incredibly similar.

From this pre-racial, pre-religious society of a couple thousand people 70,000 years ago to a multi-racial, secular society of 10 billion in 2050, the challenge remains similar: How do we develop moral and ethical frameworks to guide the development of the systems and structures in which we live?

Expanding the marketplace of ideas and ethics to equally include a variety of cultures, races and traditions should yield, from a purely evolutionary perspective, better philosophies and stronger social cohesion versus a society that requires assimilation into one dominant culture.

In many ways, the vision of a post-racial society uncompromised by institutional dogma holds great utopian promise. Imagine the sense of common purpose and shared humanity in a world where skin color and religious fealty were increasingly irrelevant. At the same time, it's also easy to envision the dystopic opposite. In a world of escalating population, diminishing resources and looming climate catastrophe, we might further bunker into competitive tribes vying for limited supplies.

Let us assume for a moment that a moral universe would yield the greatest possible flourishing of well-being (freedom, shelter, health, belonging, purpose) and minimize suffering (famine, disease, needless pain, war). This proposition emerges from consciousness as a moral intuition that is arguably universally acceptable. Can social science provide us with the empirical data that in conjunction with this moral intuition guides our behaviors and actions towards a global efflorescence of well-being? It may be that an alloying of morality and science can inform a New Enlightenment that leverages technology for the purposes of maximizing global well-being instead of corporate profits.

Science and technology will certainly be the prime drivers of the future and their ethical application will be of growing and paramount importance. Science, by its nature, must maintain value neutrality in order to be beneficial and has, to date, offered little usefulness as a framework for ethics. Perhaps the emergence of morality as a science itself, as Sam Harris posits in *The Moral Landscape*, can light the way forward. Whatever the case, this New Enlightenment must equally value reason and ethics if we are to instantiate a just society.

I know that as a meditator I should focus on the present moment but I can't help but project into the future. In 2050, assuming we make it there, I'll hopefully be in a corner somewhere, stuffed into a rocking chair, experiencing the transitory phenomena of howling grandchildren. But my daughters will be 46, 43 and 40, in the crosshairs of life. And I deeply care about what the human condition looks like, not just for my own children, but for everyone's.

Kamala Harris is a bridge into that future. How fast we get there will depend, in some measure, on how many of us follow her across this current passage. I can say, as a proud American mutt, I am willing and ready.

WRITING EXERCISES

We are all influenced by our history and heritage, or lack thereof. We all come from somewhere—the speartip of our lineage. Reflect on your relationship to your own lineage and ancestors.

Describe your family heritage and how it's influenced your identity.

What family traditions or rituals remain a part of your life? Why are they important to you?

_____

_____

_____

_____

_____

_____

_____

_____

_____

_____

What are the sources that inform your sense of morality?

_____

_____

_____

_____

_____

_____

_____

_____

_____

_____

_____

_____

_____

_____

_____

YOU SPLIT. I CHOOSE.
SEPTEMBER 6

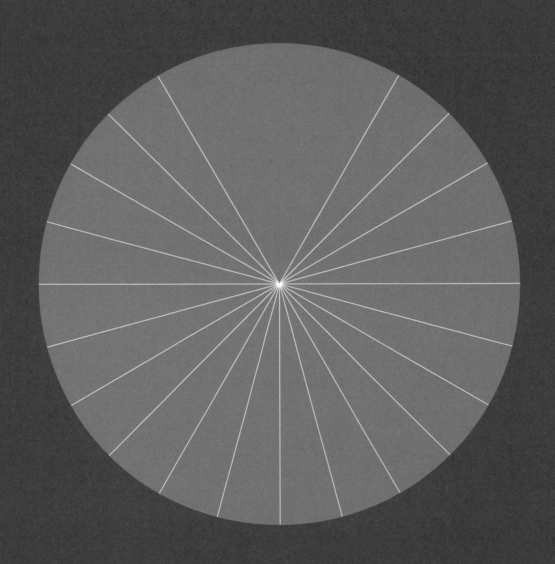

You are hosting a big party. Not right now obviously. But in the future. You must be extremely popular because heaps more people than expected are showing up. And now you're out of 7-layer bean dip, only remnant crumbs of tortilla chips litter the bottoms of bowls, and someone is licking the thin paste of remaining ranch dip off the veggie platter. You can sense a fomenting "hanger" and spring into action.

You call your local pizza joint and order the world's largest-ever pie. Fifteen minutes later, four stoned dudes (including a guy you dated in high school) show up with a twenty-foot radius pizza. They carry it in like a chuppah and drop it on your front patio. You open the box and behold a chef d'oeuvre of oozing mozzarella, fresh arugula, crisped pancetta and perfectly thin crust.

Immediately though you notice something amiss. The pizza is not sliced. And here's where this light-hearted romp becomes a philosophical conundrum.

You must cut up the pizza. *But* you don't know what piece *you* will end up with. So, how do you slice it up?

This admittedly trivial-seeming thought experiment transforms even Milton Friedman into a Marxist. Everyone, except an unrepentant slots player, converges on the same answer. They slice up the pie in equal denominations such that all party-goers are treated fairly. Let's not think the motivation is completely altruistic. People cut up the pizza equally to protect their own self-interest. Who wants to end up with a measly corner piece that's all crust (except my dad)?

In last week's screed, I prattled on extensively about how humanity will create moral frameworks in an increasingly secular society. How will we distribute wealth and power? How do we define justice and equality?

In his 1971 work, A Theory of Justice, political theorist John Rawls introduces a technique known as "The Veil of Ignorance" as a means of exploring these very concepts of morality and ethics.[21]

It follows then that the goal of an equitable society should be the ability to provide tantamount access to opportunity for all its citizens. And, if you accept this notion, then should it not also be the moral obligation of society to provide its members with a basic level of subsistence: shelter, food, health care, and education?

In the pizza instance, you are "ignorant" as to the slice you will end up with. The simplest application of the veil of ignorance technique may be the playground ritual of sharing a candy bar: You split. I choose.

When you consider societal issues more consequential than pizza or a Snickers from behind "the veil of ignorance," you don't know your class, race, gender, sexual orientation, religion, ethnicity, education and other attributes that may provide you with privilege or lack thereof. From this vantage point, one can arguably make the most unbiased and clearest determinations about justice and its application.

Mahatma Gandhi wrote, "The true measure of any society can be found in how it treats its most vulnerable members."

If there was a chance that you would be a homeless person, how would that shape your position on how we should treat the homeless? You can continue to extrapolate this concept in myriad ways. If there was a chance you might be a refugee, what would be your viewpoint on a just immigration policy? If there was a chance you might be gay, how would that impact your views on LGBTQ rights?

Humanity can ethically withstand some inequity of outcomes. For instance, someone may want to spend every breathing moment becoming a tech billionaire and someone else might prefer to seclude in the woods and pen novels. I know my predilection. But unless the world of letters becomes miraculously more lucrative, this would clearly result in financial inequity. However, this imbalance seems quite morally acceptable because the opportunity to make the decision that leads to the outcome is equally provided.

It follows then that the goal of an equitable society should be the ability to provide tantamount access to opportunity for all its citizens. And, if you accept this notion, then should it not also be the moral obligation of society to provide its members with a basic level of subsistence: shelter, food, health care, and education?

Essentially, everyone should enter life with approximately the same-sized wedge of pizza, a slice that represents one's basic needs. No true meritocracy can exist without the provision of a rudimentary level of stability from which one's well-being can flourish. In essence, a just society calibrates for arbitrary luck, compensating for the mere chance that one is born into some form of hardship or disadvantaged circumstance. And, indeed, this is what many societies endeavor to do, with varying results.

The United Nations World Happiness Reports show that the happiest people are concentrated in Northern Europe.[22] The Nordic countries (Denmark, Sweden, Norway and Finland) ranked highest on the metrics of real GDP per capita, healthy life expectancy, having someone to count on, perceived freedom to make life choices, generosity and freedom from corruption.

The Nordic model is a snuggly form of capitalism characterized by competitive free markets tempered by an elaborate social safety net which provides free education, universal health care and public pensions. There is significant public spending, hovering around 50% of GDP, and a large percentage of the population is employed by the public sector.

To Americans, the Nordic model reeks of democratic "socialism" – a word one dare not whisper without the risk of being all caps excoriated. Still, many of us in the United States recognize that the sharper edges of capitalism need dulling. Medicare, Medicaid, social security, unemployment benefits, worker's compensation; these sacred cow programs are part of a social contract that recognizes the ethical necessity of public assistance. Further, while Americans treasure their rugged individualism and cut-throat capitalism, there is growing antipathy across party lines for escalating levels of income inequality. The combined wealth of

Jeff Bezos, Bill Gates and Warren Buffett is greater than the aggregate wealth of the bottom 50% of Americans.

The American argument, one largely supported by Rawls, maintains that free-market capitalism can bake such a big pizza that even the smallest piece should provide subsistence, if not prosperity.

Much of equality and fairness can be seen through the lens of distributive justice, how we disperse what Rawls dubs our primary social goods. When humans work cooperatively together, they generate surplus. For example, Amazon is the second largest employer in the United States. They own Ring, Twitch, Whole Foods, Audible and IMDb. This mammoth staff of over 1,000,000 people works together to create surplus value in the form of corporate profits and stock value. How is this excess divvied up?

Business Insider put a microscope to Jeff Bezos' annual earnings spanning a twelve-month period between October 2017 and 2018. Per hour, Bezos made $8,961,187 ($149,353 per minute!), roughly 315 times Amazon's $28,466 median annual worker pay.[23] One might justify Bezos' wealth if it were leveraged for the overall benefit of society. The idea that inequality can be just if it benefits the aggregate is known at the "difference principle." In other words, if Bezos was utilizing his mass fortune to address deforestation in the real Amazon then we might ethically assent to such lopsided wealth distribution, but there is little indication that he is doing so.

The stratification of wealth in America is so pronounced that it led Yale Law professor, Daniel Markovitz, to point out that French Laundry, Thomas Keller's obscenely upscale bistro, and Taco Bell, the ubiquitous fast-Mexican dive, do not share a single common ingredient on their menu. Not even the salt.

Despite this universally despised asymmetry, America cannot manage to muster an intellectually honest conversation about income inequality. Any sincere attempt elicits cries of communism from conservatives and whimpers of ambivalence from centrist democrats. Bernie Sanders and Elizabeth Warren, both now fundamentally specks in the rearview mirror, were not agitating for nationalization of private assets or collective ownership of businesses. Their core message centered around adopting many of the compassionate capitalistic governing principles of the Nordic countries with the goal of creating greater equality of opportunity.

In 2009, Kate Pickett and Richard Wilkinson published The Spirit Level: Why More Equal Societies Almost Always Do Better.[24] The book highlights the pernicious effects that inequality has on societies: eroding trust, increasing anxiety and illness, and encouraging excessive consumption. It shows that for each of eleven different health and social problems: physical health, mental health, drug abuse, education, imprisonment, obesity, social mobility, trust and community life, violence, teenage pregnancies, and child well-being, outcomes are significantly worse in more unequal rich countries. It doesn't take a social scientist to map these crises squarely onto American life.

One of the most difficult concepts for people to grok is the notion that self-interest and collective good are generally one and the same thing. But one must look no further than the happiness metrics of the Nordic countries for an affirmation of this confluence.

If we care about distributive justice and instantiating a fair society then there is a lot of common ground to be found in tackling wealth inequality. Increasingly, a smaller number of people are hoarding colossal pizzas while the rest scrap for crusts. This is the real Pizzagate.

WRITING EXERCISES

Take some time to step behind Rawl's "veil of ignorance" where you don't have any identity connected to gender, race, class, sexual orientation, religious or political affiliation. From this place, outline your vision for a just society as it pertains to wealth distribution, and human rights.

How does this vision translate to policies relating to criminal justice, immigration, civil rights and other salient societal issues?

Write down the key attributes of a fair and just society. How would you measure societal happiness?

ANTISOCIAL MEDIA
SEPTEMBER 20

"Come on, honey, not at the dinner table."

Anyone with a teenager knows what this futile request refers to. And, candidly, I raise my hand, guilty as charged, for sneaking an under-the-table peak at my Instagram between helpings.

What did we used to do in the backseat on those long family drives? Sing songs? Play the alphabet game? Just be bored?

Now, we furnish our beloved progeny with glowing screens that stream endless cat videos and much worse. And they can't put them down. Of course, while they may never listen to us, they never fail to imitate us. How many of us "grown-ups" routinely and mindlessly grab for our devices within five minutes of waking up?

Be honest. But don't be too hard on yourself. You may be convinced of your own free will. But remember what you're up against. Deep Blue, a computer developed by IBM, beat Garry Kasparov in chess despite the fact that he had been playing since he was seven and reigned as world champion for twenty years. And that was in 1997, a year prior to the founding of Google. Imagine the supercomputer your self-determination is vying against now.

Since I'll spend the balance of our time together indicting social media for fostering loneliness, diminishing self-esteem, decreasing attention spans and tribalizing society, let me summarize some of its positive attributes first. Social media has given people voice, particularly the marginalized. It's a brilliant and protean tool for organization, from the Arab Spring to Lolli's wretched roller-skating party. It is an outlet for creativity, democratizing its distribution. And, of course, I love keeping up with old high school buddies and their Pomeranians (well, most of them).

The intention of social media was to enhance life, to foster connection in an increasingly individuated world. Unfortunately, its existence is a good case for consequentialism since it can be argued that nothing has atomized and polarized us more than the invective of Twitter, Facebook and YouTube.

The intention of social media was to enhance life, to foster connection in an increasingly individuated world. Unfortunately, its existence is a good case for consequentialism since it can be argued that nothing has atomized and polarized us more than the invective of Twitter, Facebook and YouTube.

A couple of statistics to grok the scale of social media usage. Facebook currently has 2.7 billion "users" – a term that the recent documentary "The Social Dilemma" points out is otherwise reserved for consumers of drugs. Facebook has added 100 million accounts in each of the last two quarters. YouTube has 2 billion users. 79% of all internet users have their own YouTube account. Teenagers clock an average of 7 hours and 22 minutes of media screen time daily – NOT including time spent using screens for school and homework.[25] While this barely seems feasible given a day consists of 1440 minutes, the typical cellphone user touches his or her phone 2,617 time every day. A study found that extreme cellphone abusers touch their devices more than 5,400 times daily.[26]

What transpires while we scan the endless scroll of phantoms held in our palms while often disregarding the three-dimensional beings in the room who we purportedly love?

Increasingly, brands use social media to market their products. You barely need to slide your index finger to be bombarded with images of unattainable perfection, six-pack abdominals and luxury getaway packages. Surfing through these targeted fantasies fosters a sense of lack or "not-enoughness." Brands then market products, services and trinkets to you to address these perceived deficiencies. And they do so with great efficacy, paying Facebook to place these images in the feeds of people who meet their demographic and psychographic profiles.

If only, and only if, I look like this and have that then I will be happy.

You don't need to be a Buddhist to comprehend that this pursuit lacks fruit. The moment you've clicked "buy now," you are already plotting your next conquest. You can't be happy in the future. Contentment is reserved for the here and now.

Perversely, social media also becomes the forum in which we trot out curated, filtered, fish-lipped renditions of our own lives. These false projections are a double-edged sword, immiserating both poster and user. In search of approval, we anxiously await the flood of likes to swell our brains with dopamine while the scroller evaluates his woeful existence against a phony portrait of flawlessness. Comparison is the invisible thief of happiness.

Neuroscientists are researching the impact of social media on the brain and discovering that positive interactions (such as someone liking your yoga selfie) trigger the same kind of chemical reaction that is caused by recreational drugs. To better understand our addiction to social media, one can draw on the work of American behavioral psychologist B. F. Skinner, who posited that actions which are reinforced tend to be repeated. Positive reinforcement strengthens a behavior by providing a consequence that is rewarding. For example, when you get a social media notification, your brain delivers a neurotransmitter called dopamine along a reward pathway that makes you flush with joy. The same phenomenon is also associated with exercise, sex, food, gambling and drugs – which can all become addictive when abused. Variable reward schedules up the stakes. When rewards are delivered randomly (like when a flurry of digital hearts light up your post) and checking for the reward is easy, the dopamine-triggering behavior becomes a subconscious habit.

In terms of understanding the ramifications of the global and nonconsensual psychological experiment of social media, we are barely glimpsing the tip of an iceberg. Here are some disturbing correlations. There is growing evidence social media increases loneliness and depression.[27] Recent surveys indicate 73% of heavy social media users consider themselves lonely.[28] The pressures of social media appear to be particularly severe for teenage girls. Teenage suicide rates for girls since 2009 have grown 70% (and 151% for girls 10 – 14). Similar increases apply for non-fatal hospital admissions among the same cohorts.[29]

The impacts of habitual overuse of social media on our personal wellness is alarming, but the deleterious impact on our societal well-being may be even greater.

Society has become increasingly politically polarized and tribalized. Forty years ago, less than 25% of us lived in landslide districts, where one candidate won in a landslide over another. Now that number is 80%. We've bunkered ourselves in echo chambers so resonant that often all we hear are modifications of our own voice. Our ability to have healthy public discourse has eroded and debate on social media almost always devolves into all caps screaming matches that only further divide and dehumanize.

How does social media contribute to extremism and the widespread espousal of unfounded theories? This quote from tech philosopher, Jaron Lanier, succinctly sums up social media's core endeavor:[30]

"It's the gradual, slight, imperceptible change in your own behavior and perception that is the product."

The modification of your ideas and how you act upon them are the product of this industry. This is what marketers, candidates, rogue groups and special interests are paying companies like Facebook and YouTube to do. The primary key performance indicator for YouTube is watch time. The more time you spend in the YouTube ecosystem the more ads they can serve up. The average visit length on YouTube is 40 minutes and the algorithm is optimized to keep you there for as long as possible.

YouTube garners approximately 1 billion hours of watch time per day according to Guillaume Chaslot, an artificial intelligence (AI) expert and former Google engineer.[31] More than 70% of views come from YouTube's recommendation engine. These personalized recommendations appear as thumbnails in the right margin on your desktop or below your video window on your mobile phone.

The recommendations are personalized for you through AI that tracks your every view and the digital behavior of others like you. This may seem innocuous enough if you are like me, searching for Mooji meditations and getting served up Eckart Tolle or Deepak Chopra.

Unfortunately, it's often significantly more insidious. For example, Chaslot reports that YouTube's algorithm detected an outlier trend that a small subsection of people watching fitness videos were also interested in pedophilia. So, it began serving up pedophilia videos among the recommendations while people were watching their high intensity interval trainings. It turns out the watch time of these lurid videos is quite high. And it appears that, in general, there is a correlation between extreme content and longer watch times. The algorithm is just doing what it is designed to do: keep people on the platform as long as possible. The problem with AI is the complete absence of moral filter. There is no ethical arbiter between creator and viewer.

The algorithm is just doing what it is designed to do: keep people on the platform as long as possible. The problem with AI is the complete absence of moral filter. There is no ethical arbiter between creator and viewer.

Fake news, which may include spurious conspiracies, proliferates across social media at a rate 6 times the truth.[32] The content is often scandalous and elicits emotions or disgust. The value-neutral algorithm's affinity for sensationalist content may be the primary reason for the explosion of unfounded theories and movements like QAnon. Alex Jones, the founder of InfoWars, was a primary propagator of theories such as Pizzagate and Birtherism, and that 9/11 and the Sandy Hook massacre were hoaxes. Before he was de-platformed by YouTube, his videos were recommended at minimum 15 billion times. It is no wonder some of these ideas have taken hold.

I have little idea how much revenue (if any) YouTube or Alex Jones generated from these video views. However, at a $5 CPM (cost per thousand views), 1 billion views would yield 5 million dollars. YouTube keeps 45% of this revenue and passes the balance to the creator. There is a financial incentive for social media to trade in dangerous and often specious content.

Many people no longer get their news from establishment sources. The endless drone of "fake news" has undermined trust in traditional media. And some of this skepticism is certainly valid. Increasingly, though, people are finding their news on social media from unreliable sources including phony news channels, celebrities and influencers, who may have good intentions, but little training in journalistic ethics. Influencers, often unwittingly, peddle weaponized misinformation and subsequently become funnels for more nefarious groups looking to undermine democracy and spread chaos. Sometimes it would be funny if it weren't so dangerous. Like the Tik Tok influencer who went viral with a post claiming that the recent West coast wildfires were planned, as evidenced by the fact that they stopped at the US-Canadian border. She was referring to a US-only databased map. She is reported to have 2 million followers.

Persuasive technology, algorithmically gamed against us, can make us feel as though we are "doing the research" and developing our own opinions. However, behavioral modification is often imperceptible to the user.

The proliferation of misinformation is aided and abetted by the algorithms. You can run this experiment yourself. For example, watch a Bill Maher or Robert Kennedy Jr. video about anti-vaccination on YouTube. Both of these gentlemen are whip smart, if sometimes too smart, and raise legitimate concerns about this issue. (As an aside, my wife points out – and I agree – that it is often the inability of the mainstream press to have intelligent public discourse on deserved topics that can push folks further toward the fringes). If you watch these vaccine-skeptical videos for a few days, like them and comment on them, you will start to be fed new video recommendations. Maybe an anti-mask wearing video. Maybe a "report" that COVID fatalities are exaggerated. If you engage with this content, the recommendation engine will progressively serve up more tantalizing fare, until you're suddenly watching a 40-minute diatribe about the Archons, an inter-dimensional race of reptilian beings who have hijacked the earth.

Slowly, invisibly, Lanier's thesis takes root. Persuasive technology, algorithmically gamed against us, can make us feel as though we are "doing the research" and developing our own opinions. However, behavioral modification is often imperceptible to the user.

I joked with Schuyler that if you espouse the theory that, through a mandated vaccine, we'll all be microchipped such that our whereabouts and proclivities will be surveilled by an elite cabal trying to instantiate a new world order then we can all relax. We already pay $1000 for a device and $100 per month voluntarily for this privilege. There is a server whirring in some non-descript bunker that knows me better than my wife of 32 years, and perhaps better than I even know myself. And access to this knowledge of who I am is being sold. This is the perhaps the "conspiracy" behind all the others.

Enough doom and gloom already. The key to addressing the deleterious impacts of social media in your own life is found in a familiar place: Awareness.

I have touted "The Social Dilemma" numerous times in this screed. It is a documentary chock-full of former Silicon Valley executives blowing whistles with the goal of spreading consciousness about social media. The Center for Humane Technology led by co-founder Tristan Harris created this documentary and is dedicated to articulating the problem and the path forward towards a new era of truly humane tech.

In the meantime, here are my humble suggestions for navigating social media consumption and happiness:

- Meditate. It will help you stay present, conscious and aware.

- Actively cultivate in-person face-to-face time wherever possible.

- Engage in nuanced, respectful conversation, especially with folks with whom you do not agree.

- Find ethical sources for news that that rely on legitimate experts and multiple sources, independently fact-check, have minimal biases, and publish corrections.

- Read or listen to long-form content that can capture nuance and expand attention span.

- Be aware of modifications and radicalizations in your own behavior and ideologies.

- And … limit your social media time. Turn off the wi-fi at night. Put your phones in a basket during dinner.

- Be present for each other.

WRITING EXERCISES

Social media has impacted everyone's existence, regardless of whether or not you use it. If you do, take some time to reflect on the impact it's had on your life.

Do you judge yourself on the basis of followers, likes or comments?

_____

_____

_____

_____

How many true friends would you have in the complete absence of social media?

_____

_____

_____

_____

_____

_____

_____

What defines those relationships?

_____

_____

_____

_____

_____

_____

_____

_____

_____

_____

_____

_____

_____

_____

_____

_____

How much of your news do you get from social media?

_____

_____

_____

_____

_____

_____

_____

Think back over the past year. How have your opinions evolved, perhaps imperceptibly, because of social media?

If social media ceased to get exist, what would be your sources for trustworthy information?

SMALL IS BEAUTIFUL

SEPTEMBER 27

I fell asleep last Thursday night, a copy of E. F. Schumacher's *Small Is Beautiful* on my chest, only to be jostled out of reverie by what I perceived to be an earthquake. In retrospect, the jolt could have been the seismic gyrations of my sister-in-law, who was in throes of labor just a mile away. In the wee hours of Friday morning, Lewis Kofi Krasno entered the world, trading seats with Justice Ginsburg. Amidst the political chaos, the fires, the virus, the uncertainty, life miraculously presses on.

To behold this unadulterated innocence in your arms is to understand that indeed small is beautiful. This radiant helpless creature, fresh from the oneness of the womb, is closer to God than I'll ever be, for he knows not the individuated self. He knows only connection. There will be a moment, probably in two years, when he will realize that he is not his mother. And, some years after that, he will become painfully aware of his own mortality and that of his parents. The double-edged sword of consciousness will be unsheathed. He will spend the rest of his life wandering, searching for this condition that he now inhabits, free of the conceptual mind, just being in the everlasting now.

My girls love babies. Even Micah dons the sling and totes little Lewis confidently around the living room so the adults can gossip. Lauren, the luminous mother, slurps the foam off her first Guinness and regales us with her birth story. Lewis is her first child and the labor was remorseless. From the blissful vantage of our snuggly dinner, she recounts the litany of obscenities shrieked between contractions. And we laugh now in direct proportion to her prior agony, as if to bring the world into emotional balance. I remember holding Schuyler, my arms bulging underneath hers, while she pushed. This act is so viscerally profound, so acutely personal that it is impossible to comprehend that it has transpired 108 billion times.

Why is being human - from delivery to demise - so painful, physically and psychologically? I don't want to belittle the plight of the mare but, in comparison to human nativity, a newborn horse is foaled with minor difficulty and, generally, unassisted. The young filly wobbles for a mere moment and then she clumsily ambles off while humans nurse off their parents' resources in an endlessly protracted and tortured tenure.

Patriarchal Christian society would blame Eve for this trouble. She desired what was forbidden and tempted her husband into willful sin. This malevolent disruption of God's plan resulted in Genesis 3:16: "To the woman He said, 'I will greatly multiply your pain in childbirth. In pain you will bring forth children; Yet your desire will be for your husband, and he will rule over you." Indicting Eve for women's perennial suffering is patently unfair. This mythology also fosters fear. And, if there's one thing I have learned after three rounds, fear is the enemy of the birthing room.

The success of our species is predicated on our ability to cooperate flexibly at scale. And this human skill may be a product of our need for collective child-rearing. Certainly not every child is born into a loving community, but those who are gain a birthright of inestimable advantage.

Though I have no plans to breastfeed Lewis, I am reminded of how much I like Guinness. And while I am completely sober scrawling this text now, I did originally posit this potentially ridiculous theory under some influence. I have subsequently learned that this thesis is actually known as the obstetrical dilemma. It involves a number of opposing evolutionary pressures including bipedalism and increased cranium size.

The timelines of these evolutionary developments are murky. However, it appears as if our hominid ancestors, the aptly named Homo erectus, got firmly on their two feet some 1.9 million years ago. Human hips tapered to support locomotion. Male and female hips evolved differently both from a size and angle perspective as women needed to be able to carry out the process of childbirth and also be able to move bipedally. In fact, examination of the pelvis proves to be the most useful method for identifying biological sex using the skeleton.

Early Homo erectus had modestly sized brains, approximately 600 cubic centimeters. However, cranium size doubled over time. One possible explanation for this development relates to the domestication of fire. Somewhere around 500,000 years ago, it is believed that humans got quite proficient at harnessing fire for the purpose of cooking. There is evidence of ancient hearths and earthen ovens dating back 300,000 years.

Cooking added a number of new pages to the human menu. Meat could now be grilled and vegetables could be softened through boiling. Other delights, heretofore inedible, like grains and root vegetables, could now be prepared for consumption. It is substantially easier to digest cooked food. Think of the chimp who monastically spends hours upon hours masticating leaves. There is evidence to suggest that cooked food diminished the amount of energy the body needed to digest, thereby reducing the length of human intestines. The body then directed this newly-found excess energy toward the brain. The average size of the Homo sapien brain is 1400 cubic centimeters. Hence, the dilemma: narrower birth canal meets bigger brain in an epic evolutionary clash.

One possible compromise between these countervailing forces was a truncated gestation period. There is some anthropogenic data suggesting there was once a "fourth trimester" that provided additional development time in the womb. But that through an evolutionary imperative to accommodate our ever-expanding cranium, human babies needed to born "pre-maturely." This would explain why our cherubic children are such helpless, if loveable, blobs at birth.

While this is an amusing rant at a dinner party, I can't completely stand behind the science. And, now, I have read accounts that contradict pieces of this narrative. However, regardless of the evolutionary explanation, human babies are inarguably less self-sufficient than virtually any other mammals' progeny. They require constant attention, feeding and tutelage. The prolific needs of our young children have had significant impact on our social structures. The well-worn African proverb,

"It takes a village to raise a child" suggests that an entire community of people must interact with children to insure their well-being. We need Gramma to help out (but not too much!). We need friends and neighbors to take shifts, mash avocados and share the burden.

The success of our species is predicated on our ability to cooperate flexibly at scale. And this human skill may be a product of our need for collective child-rearing. Certainly not every child is born into a loving community, but those who are gain a birthright of inestimable advantage.

The other dimension of our prolonged development relates to identity. Human children remain highly impressionable for an extended period. Parents and community have enormous influence over who we think we are. Virtually all Catholics hold their specific faith because their parents are Catholic. The same logic applies for any religion, political affiliation, language, opinion, diet and so on. It's not until we get pimples and become malodorous that we remotely question what we believe in and why. We are convinced that we shape our world. Yet, so often, we are shaped by it. The awareness of our programming, imprinted not just by our parents, but also by our culture, rituals and media, often begets a personal reckoning. There is inevitably a solitary and reflective moment where we ask, "Who the hell am I?"

After three daughters and two nieces, I am over the moon to have a nephew, to engage in all the archetypal rituals of manhood; throwing footballs, going to games, drinking beer, telling dumb jokes. I know he's but a week old, but is it ever too early to stock up on fishing tackle and poker chips? Or perhaps a broadening culture will afford him the opportunity to eschew these tired tropes of masculinity and hop in the dance class carpool with his cousins.

I am thrilled for my brother, Eric, and Lauren as they enter this delicious phase of life. I am delighted for my father that the Krasno name has precariously squeaked by into another generation. But I bear the same fears, and no small measure of guilt, for Sweet Lew that I shoulder for my own children. Nothing makes the global mayhem we have wrought more palpable then when we witness it through the prism of our children. We feel the hot breath of looming environmental catastrophe, vitriolic polarization and the unraveling of social cohesion on our necks. I have crested the summit and am now headed home. But, Lew, he'll inherit what's left. And if there's anything in the world that should inspire us to live peacefully with each other and the planet, it is the glorious emergence of new life. It is he, small and beautiful.

THE MIDDLE WAY

OCTOBER 4

Close your eyes. Sit tall, with your back straight. Plant your feet solidly on the ground below you. Take a deep breath in through your nose.

And hold it until November 3. Probably longer.

Shut-eye doesn't come easy right now, thoughts are swinging from branch to branch like a monkey. That debate debacle bore some semblance to the chatterbox in my head, where two imaginary frenemies incessantly prattle over each other:

"Please go to sleep.
Why didn't you go to the bathroom before you lay down?
You really seem to be going a lot.
God, maybe you have diabetes?
Or maybe it's a prostate thing?
You're such a hypochondriac.
Still, you should probably go see the doctor.
But he moved.
Yeah, that motherf**ker moved.
You never really liked him and you should find someone on the east side.
The east side is much hipper anyways.
Yeah, better restaurants.
The west side is so ... Gwyneth.
Screw Goop.
I like the Politician, though."

If this inner dialogue was amplified out of my mouth, you would consider me certifiably insane. Yet, too often, such is the chaos of our psyche.

After I have tamed my cortisol-fueled hysteria with half-a-dozen CBD gummies and rubbed lavender copiously on my temples, I drift in and out of a restless slumber. I roll around fitfully, obsessing over my latest Facebook troll, conjuring come-backs. Really, Jeff? After all the meditation and tiresome exercises in self-transcendence, concocting social media barbs is how you're going to spend your brief time of this planet?

Breathe. Count backwards from one hundred.

And then, like Rip Van Winkle, I am lucid. It's November 28 and my girls have baked me a cock-eyed carrot cake. They are singing happy birthday painfully if beautifully off-pitch. I stroke my long white beard. A cool rain blankets the gilded hills of California. And democracy is preserved.

Of course, the real dream is that this dream is not a dream.

Back in the frenetic custody of the moment, we find ourselves utterly polarized. Have you ever pulled a fraying shoelace from each end, eyeing the middle as it unravels, until there's a mere single strand tenuously and bravely holding communion? This is our country. One eye shut in denial, one eye reticently open, the undertow pulling us out into a choppy uncivil war.

The vase of truth lies shattered on the floor. We are but millions of shards of individuated and machine-curated modifications of an unshared existence. It's no wonder we debase and not debate. Silicon Valley serves up a different feed of reality to each one of us. How can we cooperate without a shared foundational understanding of fact? And, now, the sane among us must take on the project of gluing together some semblance of inter-subjective reality.

The problem is that truth ain't dressed in a mini-skirt. It won't be propagated through memes. Truth is not sensational. It doesn't go viral. It lives in the thicket of nuance, in the gray zone.

In the very first lesson Gautama Buddha delivered after his awakening, he spoke of the middle path. In this sutra, Buddha describes the Noble Eightfold Path as the middle way of moderation, a life between the extremes of any polarity as objective reality.

The middle way is the course we must chart, as we sense the emergence of a new paradigm. In this moment of profound instability, there is the potential for substantial progress. We are questioning our systems and structures, putting a microscope to institutions that have long provided stability, sometimes at the expense of justice and equality. But here we must use discernment between baby and bathwater.

For example, we should hold the "mainstream" media to account for its many shortcomings. But let us remember that these many outlets

The middle way is the course we must chart, as we sense the emergence of a new paradigm. In this moment of profound instability, there is the potential for substantial progress. We are questioning our systems and structures, putting a microscope to institutions that have long provided stability, sometimes at the expense of justice and equality. But here we must use discernment between baby and bathwater.

compete with one another. There is no solitary cigar-smoking pluto-crat directing them all à la Operation Mockingbird. Still, the insidious ad-revenue model that rewards sensationalism and hyperbole dribbles a popcorn trail to the extremes. The 24-hour news cycle values speed over depth. Misaligned incentives propel biased reporting. And the inability of many outlets to platform legitimate issues can push us to the thin edges of the branch.

Still, though, we must recognize the utility of journalism to hold government, the private sector, and bad actors to account. In 1972, Woodward and Bernstein, reporters for The Washington Post, led the investigative work that shed light on the Watergate scandal and precipitated the eventual resignation of President Nixon. In 1984, Bob Parry and Brian Barger broke the Iran-Contra Affair for the Associated Press. In 2002, a scrappy team from the Boston Globe uncovered cases of widespread and systemic child sex abuse in the Boston area by numerous Roman Catholic priests. This work was chronicled in the award-winning film, Spotlight. In 2003, former diplomat Joseph Wilson called out the non-existence of weapons of mass destruction in Iraq in a New York Times op-ed. In 2018, Miami Herald reporters, Julie K. Brown and Emily Michot did the harrowing work of reviving the Jeffrey Epstein case, which had been cold for a decade. The Pulitzer Prize-winning series "Perversion of Justice" not only took down Epstein but also unveiled profound culpabilities in our criminal justice system. And, right now, the most comprehensive work to expose child pornography and hold

Big Tech to account is being done by Gabriel Dance and his investigative team at the New York Times.

I could spend the better part of a day recounting the myriad instances that hard-nosed journalism unearthed malfeasance, bringing bad actors to justice. This work is heroic and, more often than not, unheralded. It is being done for meager financial reward and at great personal risk by women and men rigorously committed to exhuming the truth.

In 2015, Washington Post foreign correspondent, Jason Rezaian spent 544 days in an Iranian prison where he was informed daily of his impending execution.[33] His colleague, Jamal Khashoggi, who had been sharply critical of Saudi Arabia's crown prince, Mohammad bin Salman, wasn't so lucky. He was assassinated at the Saudi consulate in Istanbul on October 2, 2018 by agents of the Saudi government and cut up into small pieces.[34] This courageous and often overlooked work is pitted against YouTube, which recommended the spurious videos of Alex Jones over 15 billion times. The migration of news to social media represents the divorce of power and responsibility.

My point is that – in evaluating our institutions, and, perhaps, life in general – there is a middle way that both recognizes good and bad, useful and broken, transcendent and redeemable. By moderating our own attitudes around a golden mean, we can focus on the betterment of these very systems.

Clearly, some of the caffeine has worn off along with the humor. Time for a refill.

I am no cheerleader for Western allopathic medicine or its villainous cousin, Big Pharma. I tend to dabble in alternative remedies and a good amount of Krasnopathy, the emerging field of sweeping ailments under the rug until they go away. A white coat generally reduces me to a puddle of nerves. But I can tell you that, right now, given that I have just returned home from excruciating dental work, I am grabbing my pom-poms and doing splits for that anesthesiologist.

Yes, there is a parade of examples of Big Pharma negligence. The Merck arthritis drug, Vioxx, was responsible for giving 38,000 people fatal heart attacks.[35] Purdue Pharma persisted in marketing OxyContin even though it was aware of its addictive and deleterious impacts.[36]

This drug ignited the opioid crisis that has taken 500,000 American lives. Denvaxia, a vaccine designed to prevent dengue, actually exacerbated severe symptoms and increased the risk of a deadly complication called plasma leakage syndrome with children in the Philippines.[37] Gerald Ford's rushed and botched H1N1 vaccine led to an estimated 450 people developing the paralyzing syndrome Guillain-Barré and of those, more than 30 died.[38]

For all these horrific shortcomings (and scores more), we can also celebrate the achievements of science and Western medicine that have greatly alleviated human suffering. 300 million people died of smallpox in the 20th century alone. This ravaging disease was declared completely eliminated in 1980. The discovery and development of the aforementioned anesthesia (1846), germ theory (1861), medical imaging (1895), penicillin (1928), organ transplants (1954), stem cell research (1970's) and HIV therapy (2000's), to name a few, have cured infections, prolonged life and minimized needless misery.

On a personal note, as a young boy, I spent hard times in the pediatric ward of Sloane-Kettering. And my father is currently recovering from colon cancer. I am *both* committed to living a healthy lifestyle *and* profoundly grateful for those who have devoted their lives to cancer research.

I use the institutions of media and medicine as examples as they are currently in the crosshairs of the polemic. However, you might apply the same thought exercise to any number of systems governed by humans. The media is populated by journalists, medicine is inhabited by physicians and scientists. And people are highly imperfect.

But as we imagine the world our hearts desire, will we let perfect be the enemy of good?

Or can we stand in what T.S. Eliot called "the still point of the turning world"? In the same way that higher consciousness requires us to float above our perceived selves as witnesses, to be aware of our own awareness, our collective consciousness demands a similar discipline: an ability to discern from a place of non-duality.

Many of us are so obsessively staring at screens twelve inches from our faces that we seldom look up. But when we hike up the hill of consciousness, we open the aperture of our awareness and, from this vantage, witness the broadest swath of our humanity, warts and all. From here, we can commit to the right work, the right action, the right speech – the noble path – that slowly bends the moral arc of history.

As we descend back into our villages to chop the wood and carry the water of life, the middle way beckons.

WRITING EXERCISES

Reflect upon your strongest-held opinions. Oftentimes, our convictions are grounded in thoughtful contemplation. However, many issues are extremely complex, nuanced and cannot be framed in black and white terms.

Where in your belief structure is there room for moderation?

What systems and structures are flawed but worthy of saving through improvement?

What personal habits could benefit from adopting a middle path?

THE 'RONA
OCTOBER 11

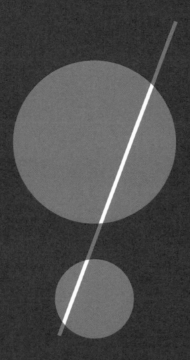

In mid-September, national hero Ruth Bader Ginsberg passed away and mourners gathered around the country to hold vigils for the late Justice. Republican's pressed forward to quickly confirm Amy Coney Barret, the conservative replacement nominee, as the new Supreme Court Justice. As the election neared, Trump continued to hold indoor rallies without masks, minimizing the deaths of now 200,000 Americans to covid-19. Soon, a litany of government representatives that were attending a White House event tested positive for the coronavirus. At 1am on Friday October 1st, President Trump tweeted that he had tested positive for the virus, After 4 days at Walter Reed Military Hospital, where he had access to the best care in the world and emerging covid-19 treatments, he was released, quickly dismissing the severity of the threat of the virus.

In mid-February 2020, my friend Russell and I attended a conference called The Conscious Life Expo. The twisted irony of the name will whistle out the kettle in a moment.

The event was hosted at the LAX Hilton, a nondescript concrete behemoth beside the Los Angeles airport. Behind the banal façade, like a technicolor pearl in an oyster, an animated psychedelia awaited.

As we entered through the sliding glass, the scene was like a new age rendition of the Star Wars cantina bar. Hundreds of henna-tattooed droids and crystal-necklaced wookies sipped Starbucks' dark roast while lathering on essential oils. Dread-locked hippies twirled to the wails of Waheguru in front of a makeshift stage in the marble lobby.

Russell is tall and, candidly, famous so we donned our hoods, like two Jawas, and surreptitiously slinked around the periphery of the mayhem.

We slithered up the stairs and into the entrails of the marketplace as if performing a spiritual colonoscopy of the conference center. The bazaar was sardined with every sort of mystic, sage and seeker hocking their wares; dreamcatchers and didgeridoos, palo santo and hemp leggings, books on finding yourself and others on losing yourself. Apparently, black tourmaline sends energy down through the root chakra and out the earth star chakra beneath your feet. Who knew?

The jammed hallways, the dropped cottage cheese ceiling and Russell's height coalesced into panic-inducing claustrophobia like we were on Malkovich's seventh-and-a-half floor. Finally, we were squirted into the world's most diminutive conference room where Russell was booked to speak.

People swarmed in. Extra chairs were filled as quickly as they were added. A bejeweled lady with purple hair snuggled in next to me and produced not one, but two small parakeets from her satchel, each balanced on a shoulder. I'm not kidding you. In a Hilton!

Uncertainty is not the friend of the conceptual mind. When the mind cannot know, it will often default to fear over love, to reactivity over responsiveness. How many of us have been living in this exhausted, anxious, agitated, cortisol-fueled state, desperately trying to know the unknowable?

As people waited for Russell, it felt like a plane taxiing to the runway, revving for lift-off. Attendees began coughing like an orchestra tuning up before the concert, high-pitched short hacks coming from the piccolo, low resonant croaks from the bassoon. A cosmic pestilence filled the air like a fog machine.

Russell dazzled as per usual, gave me a look, and from the petri dish we squiggled. It was as if the Expo sneezed and propelled us like droplets out the mouth of the sliding doors and back into dull care. I'd never been happier to see a banker in a pin-striped suit hailing an Uber.

Knackered, I trudged home and went immediately to sleep.

I woke up the next day, a Sunday, and felt off. My throat was scratchy and my chest was tight. My condition deteriorated over the course of the day. By Monday, I was running 102 and hacking uncontrollably. My body ached like I'd run a marathon. The fatigue was so profound I could only relate it to the feeling I had in the aftermath of the many flights I took from Tokyo to New York. I remained in this acute state of illness for two weeks.

Through the entirety of March and April, as the family sheltered in place, these symptoms intermittently recurred, albeit less intensely. I'd attempt to take a walk only to turn around a hundred yards out in a clammy sweat and melt back into the puddle of my sheets. Daddy had what little Micah calls "the 'Rona."

I am not exactly Jeff "The Rock" Krasno, but I am healthy. I exercise daily and I eat well. I have none of the comorbidities associated with severe COVID-19 contraction. Despite the propellers of Marine 1 whirring outside my window, I opted for self-treatment over air-lift. Of course, we knew little about this menace in the early Spring so I followed my instincts. I alkalized my body, gargling and drinking an unimaginable amount of apple cider vinegar. I built up my microbiome with probiotic sea plankton and coconut yogurt kefir. I "sweatidated" in the sauna by pouring eucalyptus water on the searing rocks until the air was stoked to 190 degrees and then breathing deeply to the guidance of Mooji, the Jamaican spiritual teacher. I took lypo-spheric vitamin C and vitamin D. I ate clean, didn't drink alcohol, severely limited my caffeine and got outside when I felt up to it. I slowly crawled my way back into well-being, though my children claim I remain mentally deranged.

My intention is not to be cheeky, though I suppose the world might benefit from some levity. A truck backed into my immune system and dumped a viral load big enough to mulch a football pitch. I was fortunate to be able to quarantine and have the resources to self-administer myriad if cockamamie treatments. Frontline workers, health care professionals, delivery drivers, grocery clerks, scientists, meatpackers, government officials and many others could not shelter-in-place. Of those who have gotten sick, many do not have adequate health care or the resources to self-treat as I did. We owe them a great debt. And, to the best estimates, 37 million people have been diagnosed with the disease and over 1 million have died, including parents of good friends.

If you can remember back to March – and I don't blame you if you cannot given the successive deluge of world events – you'll recall how little we knew about the virus. Lying on my bed in my seventh sweat-soaked shirt of the afternoon, my phone abuzz with sensationalism, I had no choice but to lean deeply into my meditation practice or go mad. For two hours a day, I drifted into the emptiness and I am not confident I have completely returned from the void. There appears to be some sort of sacred latency between the happenings of things and my responses to them. These essays have emerged from this uninhabited space as honest attempts to better understand the world more from the perspective of a witness than a participant.

Standing behind everything that separates us, beneath the various identity costumes we wear, we share a common need for purpose, belonging and well-being. This coronavirus is a barrier between us and our personal and collective health, our ability to connect with those we love and earn a living to support our families.

Another distant memory is the halcyon moment when we imagined that a global pandemic might unite us, envisioning the virus as blind to race, class and creed. Yet viable solutions to solving the greatest challenge of the last 100 years have been shrouded in a thick political marine layer. And while it's difficult to navigate true north in a fog, still, we're all piloting theories. It doesn't help that our wacky cousin, and other more nefarious characters, are hurling misinformation at us like rotten tomatoes on Facebook. We are doom-scrolling, awash in memes and YouTube videos positing this theory and that.

Uncertainty is not the friend of the conceptual mind. When the mind cannot know, it will often default to fear over love, to reactivity over responsiveness. How many of us have been living in this exhausted, anxious, agitated, cortisol-fueled state, desperately trying to know the unknowable?

The invective of politics is so triggering that we lose our capacity for compassion and discernment. It's preposterous that our political identities have anything to do with an issue as trivial as mask-wearing. Yes, I have read about 20 studies with varying conclusions, but forget this disease even exists for a moment and return to a saner time. When I was a boy, any time I coughed or sneezed, my mum told me to cover my mouth. This was a moral lesson: I shouldn't spread my germs because I value the health of the people around me. Love thy neighbor. The Golden Rule.

When we step back from the short-fused political polemic, we often find a simpler moral intuition to guide us. We all need some time to catch our breath.

Haste and science make cranky bedfellows. Yet politics is stomping its feet for answers now. And, in this demand, science falters and equivocates, further undermining confidence in itself. Vacillations about the nature of COVID's transmissibility, for example, have confounded and confused. Good science – like good food, wine, yoga, piano playing, athleticism or art – takes time and requires patience. And good science, like those other endeavors, can bring us together. It is in togetherness, in scaled and flexible cooperation, that we achieve the great projects of humanity.

As fraught as this moment is, it is also pregnant with opportunity. If we could step back from the political precipice and on to the perennial sturdiness of morality and reason, if we could commune around a global collective effort to tame the virus, we could write a new world story.

This virus appears to be highly transmissible with a relatively low fatality rate. It more severely impacts the elderly and those with comorbidities. This is a more insidious combination than immediately apparent. Higher fatality rates, for instance, might actually staunch the spread, as the virus would incapacitate or kill its hosts with greater frequency and justify more drastic lockdown measures. But, as it is, asymptomatic carriers can bop around and bestow the illness upon the more vulnerable.

This is where an ethical and moral dilemma surfaces. Many of us have intellectually tangled with the concept of herd immunity, which propagates the idea that we entirely reopen our economies and, in short order, 60% to 70% of the population will have the antibodies and the disease will wither. Of course, we don't know how close to these percentages we currently are. Knowing, however, that the illness is more fatal among people with heart disease, obesity, diabetes and other chronic diseases, and that these conditions are highly correlated across underprivileged socio-economic (and, by extension, racial) groups, we must honestly face this question: Is it ethical to sacrifice the lives of our disadvantaged and elderly in the pursuit of herd immunity? If so, how many? The virus itself does not discriminate yet it shines a light onto where humans have.

There may be another way, a middle path. In the short term, we may see significant spikes of cases during the winter in the Northern hemisphere. But, together, we can rally around a number of measures to mitigate spread and fatalities. We can cautiously open sections of the economy and "dance in and dance out." We can practice common sense public health guidelines, which do not have to be draconian or politicized. Limit large gatherings (80% of the cases come from 10% of people). Practice personal hygiene. Bolster immune systems though public health initiatives. Institute mass testing with rapid response home tests. Where there are outbreak clusters, we tamp down and contact trace.

There is also reason for optimism on numerous anti-viral fronts. A number of therapeutics including monoclonal antibodies[39] (mAbs) (which the President received) and convalescent plasma therapy[40] (CPT) are promising treatments. CPT uses blood plasma taken from people who have recovered from COVID-19 which contains antibodies that can recognize and neutralize SARS-CoV-2 as well as other components that may contribute to an immune response. These therapies can be used prophylactically within small circles as "ring vaccination." For example, if someone within a family or social group contracts the disease, mAbs can be administered to other members within the group.

These community measures are most likely bridges to a widely distributed vaccine. Currently, there is tremendous public skepticism around a COVID vaccine, with a majority of Americans claiming they would not take it. Much of that skepticism is derived from, again, political pressure that is forcing vaccine developers and the FDA to rush a product to market. The looming election plays a prominent role in the current administration's Operation Warp Speed initiative. Some urgency is clearly productive and there appears to be significant progress among numerous drugmakers.

Still, large-scale peer reviewed clinical trials must run their course. The outcomes need to prove beyond any doubt that a vaccine is completely safe. Recently, nine prominent drug makers pledged that they will not submit vaccine candidates for FDA review until their safety and efficacy is shown in large clinical trials. The move is intended to bolster public confidence amid the rush to make a COVID-19 vaccine widely available, and counter fears of political pressure to deliver a vaccine before the November presidential election.

Skeptics with legitimate concerns will still exist, but if there is a safe vaccine available in the summer 2021, people may slowly shift their attitudes if it means they can see their families and friends, go back to work, travel and go to restaurants. Many may not decide to take the vaccine, but if approximately 70% do elect to accept it, then we may achieve herd immunity.

This is just a paltry plan from a bloke tapping keys in a guest house. But we do need some blueprint. Otherwise, we're back at that Hilton Expo, waiting for two ravens to fly past a harvest moon while a crystal refracts the light from the iris of a coyote.

We can eradicate the virus. And, in doing so, we can accomplish something greater. We can re-establish faith in the best part of the institutions that eliminated smallpox and put a man on the moon. We can eschew odious politics and rally the mighty infrastructure of our government to serve the people. We can move our collective conscious out of the amygdala, the center of fear, and into the pre-frontal cortex where sound judgment is reasoned. We can summon our better angels and grant ourselves and each other some grace. We can honor those who have passed by leveraging this hideous time into a more peaceable and global communion.

WRITING EXERCISES

At its core, COVID-19 is a public health issue. However, particularly in the United States, it has become highly politicized. Many people's beliefs about the disease have become intertwined with their political identity. Information about the disease has been cherry-picked and, in some cases, falsified to support one political narrative or another.

Take a moment to step out of the political invective and leave your preconceived notions at the door. Write down what you truly know about the disease and how we could have handled it better.

GOOD GRIEF

OCTOBER 18

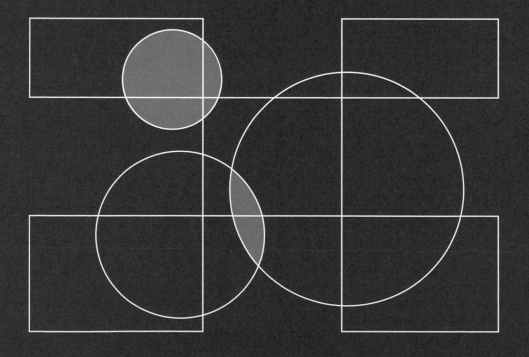

Ever since the baby was born, Terri never quite felt herself. The weight she gained during pregnancy gnawed at her. The fabric of her marriage was threadbare. Her degree in social work hung cock-eyed and dusty on the wall. She had seen a doctor who had scripted her a second-generation anti-depressant. And now it was as if there were a thin gauze layered between her and the world. Colors were muted. The clatter and buzz of the city dampened. One day, while slicing a cucumber, she nicked her middle finger. She didn't even notice until she spotted the burgundy stains on her blouse. Maybe she had married Ben too soon. Maybe she should have gone back to school as planned. Maybe. Maybe.

One August day, Terri decided to bike to Lincoln Park. She strapped little Susan into the baby seat and mounted her cruiser. The summer sun scorched. She veered right on Grant off Larrabee. The wind and the heat, the boisterous silence of the city streets, their crowded emptiness, their empty crowdedness, it spun her mind.

Where Grant met Clark, a high curb lipped the avenue. Maybe she saw it. She worked the pedals. The chain turned. The handlebars rattled. The front tire smacked the curb and Terri sailed off the bike seat. Time briefly stalled as she hovered above the madness and then floated to the asphalt with an unbearable gentleness, her mind finally clear.

As per their nightly ritual, Adeline and Arthur sat at the card table playing pinochle, two glasses of scotch sweating atop marble coasters. Back in those days, you answered the phone when it rang. Arthur trod across the room and grabbed the handset. It was Seymour. Arthur crewed with him on weekend sailing expeditions on Lake Michigan.

"Arthur, turn on the television. I think Susan is on the news."
"Adeline, turn on the TV. Seymour, I'll call you back."

Sure enough, Susan was on the 5 o'clock local news with a caption underneath that read, "If you recognize this baby, please call 312-746-6010." Adeline scrawled the number down on her score sheet.

Arthur dragged the rotary clockwise with his index finger as swiftly as he could. An administrator at the Chicago Police Department answered.

In his typical straightforward manner, he said, "This is Arthur Kaplan. My grand-daughter is on the news." There was a pause on the line. A detective grabbed the phone.

"You say your grand-daughter is on the news."
"That's right."

"Is that your daughter's daughter?"
"That's correct."
"I'm very sorry Mr. Kaplan, but I have some bad news."

———————————————

Some of my first vivid memories were of my aunt Terri. She visited us when we lived in Santiago de Compostela, Spain, in 1973. We toured the old church together and played hide-and-seek behind the massive rocks in the courtyard. She was spry and playful. My father and his brother felt an effusive, if custodial, love for their sister. But no one cherished her more than her father Arthur, my grandfather. The loss of his beloved daughter was eviscerating.

I wonder if there is any greater pain than burying a child. The confounding dis-order of never beholding the full expression of their being. Life's singular canvas torn away mid-brushstroke, a work unfinished. A redemptive hope beyond your own life dashed. The horror of it leads us to forget that, in death, the pain is often mercifully transferred from those who suffer to those who remain.

Papa, as we called him, remained outwardly stoic in his grief. He stood quietly in the pain with no umbrella. He was part of what Tom Brokaw dubbed the Greatest Generation, those who grew up during the deprivation of the Great Depression and served their country valiantly. They possessed a steely resolve, rarely showed emotion, and never wore jeans.

Being a consummate real estate man, Papa negotiated with himself in the wake of Terri's death. If only he had called that morning, been more present, provided more support, insisted she stay in school, protected her better, kept her away from that man, fill in the blank. Inevitably, against his will, he surrendered. He was bidding on a building with no address. Terri had left the bargaining table. And, in this acceptance, a benevolence toward himself cautiously emerged within him, a self-compassion. The emotional boot camp of his loss propelled a type of spiritual evolution in my grandfather.

Recognizing the suffering of another may exist along a spectrum from pity to sympathy to empathy to compassion.

Papa had little patience for pity, which he found demeaning to both provider and recipient. Sympathy may be understood as a lesser form of empathy, a cognitive and emotional acknowledgment of someone's pain but with no requirement of agency. Empathy is the donning of the emotional clothing of another, but this psychological state has no valence. It can be understood as emotional contagiousness, where someone's sadness may trigger your sadness while another's joy may elicit your own joyfulness.

Papa made the full and arduous trek and, over time, came to embody compassion—lovingkindness in the presence of another's suffering in a manner that actively seeks to alleviate that suffering. He was never morbid. On the contrary, he lived in a state of great expansiveness and generosity. For the balance of his life, he doubled down on love. He was the fulcrum of all family reunions and excursions. He put every child and grandchild through college. Adeline dubbed him Mr. Possible, because he made everything in our lives possible.

I visited Papa once in Miami. It was June, the air hot and wet. Papa woke up early, the rising sun his alarm clock. He strode to the porch, slid the glass door shut behind him and stared out over the vast ocean. I watched him for a long time from the kitchen as he stood quietly, motionless, the sun on his face. Finally, I walked out and stood beside him. He raised his hand and put it firmly on my shoulder.

"It's Terri's birthday," he said softly.

I looked at his glassy eyes still fixed upon the distant horizon. He was too proud to let me see him cry. Pulsating rhythmically on the side of my neck, his hand shed the tears. It was the only time I ever heard him utter her name. Despite the profound love he shared with all of us, the pain was still unspeakable. We filled the chasm of his heart with love's rushing water, but there remained a damned estuary where the land lay arid and fallow.

When he passed and soared above the vacillations of space and time, my sadness was tempered. He would now know what had previously been unavailable to know, why she had to leave in the manner she did.

I have been reminded recently of my grandfather's hero's journey by the approximately 6,387 daily emails I receive from Grandpa Joe asking me to "chip in $2." Somewhere tucked far beneath the curated folksiness of these robo-emails is a similar tale of grief. I ask the reader to please hover above the political invective for a moment. It will still be there when you land.

On December 18, 1972, Biden's wife, Neilia, and their three children were Christmas shopping. They all loaded in the car and were headed home, tree atop the roof, when a tractor-trailer broadsided them. Neilia and daughter, Naomi, were killed instantly. Sons Beau and Hunter sustained severe injuries. Biden, 30 years old and recently elected to his first Senate post, was in Washington. Like my grandfather, he would receive news of the tragedy on a phone call. Beau would later die in 2015 of a rare strain of brain cancer.

I make no comment on Biden's politics here but simply render this humanistic observation. He appears most authentic, most energetically at home, when providing comfort to those in pain.[41]

In her landmark work On Death and Dying, Elisabeth Kübler-Ross famously delineated the five stages of grief we experience after the loss of a loved one: denial, anger, bargaining, depression, and, finally, acceptance.[42]

In denial, by pretending the loss does not exist, we decelerate the emotional processing of the overwhelming pain.

The grief many of us experience is rarely as extraordinary as the death of a child or the Holocaust. But though our quotidian sorrows are mundane by comparison, all colors of grief are undeniably real and can cause profound anguish. The fracture of a romantic relationship, a friend moving away, the loss of a job, the sale of a family home. These realities, and a host of others, point to an unavoidable and integral component of the human condition: pain is inevitable.

In anger, we feel free to express strong emotion without vulnerability. Anger, more socially acceptable than admitting we are scared, allows us to express emotion with less fear of judgment.

In bargaining, we grope for some perceived semblance of control in a situation where none exists. We might ruminate over our interactions with the person we have lost, recall times when we may have said things we did not mean, and wish we could go back and behave differently to alleviate any pain we may have caused.

In depression, panic ebbs, the emotional marine layer burns off and the loss is visibly clear. We often pull inward, recoiling into a cocoon of mourning.

In acceptance, the pain remains visceral but we no longer resist reality and cease our attempts to pretzel it into something it is not.

Anyone who has experienced this process of grief will note that it does not unfold in linear fashion. We are tossed turbulently between these stages. We get stuck, break through and break down while slowly, inexorably, crawling towards acceptance.

In his recent book Finding Meaning, grief expert and friend David Kessler weaves a sixth stage into processing grief: purpose.

At the other end of sorrow's long, winding hallway there is a door that opens onto the opportunity to channel suffering into compassion, munificence and the betterment of the human condition. This magnanimity may take different forms. Candace Lightner, for example, founded the non-profit Mothers Against Drunk Driving (MADD) after her 13-year old daughter, Cari, was killed by an inebriated driver.

My grandfather found purpose in his unwavering commitment to family. In our quest to find redemptive meaning in loss, we make amends, forgive, launch charities, volunteer, and, even, run for president.

Man's search for meaning, as chronicled memorably in Viktor Frankl's eponymous text, can be found in three places: in love and relationships, in creative work and self-expression, and in suffering. The last category, of course, is the most challenging. In his 1946 book chronicling his experiences as a prisoner in Nazi concentration camps during World War II, Frankl takes on Freud in this remarkable passage:

"Sigmund Freud once asserted, 'Let one attempt to expose a number of the most diverse people uniformly to hunger. With the increase of the imperative urge of hunger all individual differences will blur, and in their stead will appear the uniform expression of the one unstilled urge.' Thank heaven, Sigmund Freud was spared knowing the concentration camps from the inside. His subjects lay on a couch designed in the plush style of Victorian culture, not in the filth of Auschwitz. There, the 'individual differences' did not 'blur' but, on the contrary, people became more different; people unmasked themselves, both the swine and the saints."

Frankl describes in vivid and moving detail the efforts of select prisoners to provide their last piece of bread or boots or shoelaces to those in greater need. Despite conditions unimaginable in their horror, there were those in the camps that found profound compassion, lovingkindness in the presence of pain, meaning in their suffering.

The grief many of us experience is rarely as extraordinary as the death of a child or the Holocaust. But though our quotidian sorrows are mundane by comparison, all colors of grief are undeniably real and can cause profound anguish. The fracture of a romantic relationship, a friend moving away, the loss of a job, the sale of a family home. These realities, and a host of others, point to an unavoidable and integral component of the human condition: pain is inevitable.

The psychologist Erich Fromm wrote, "To spare oneself from grief at all cost can be achieved only at the price of total detachment, which excludes the ability to experience happiness." In short, to know grief is to love.

Would we have it any other way?

I likely don't know you, but I am confident in this. Every single person reading this text has a story that would turn me inside out and make me weep. We are unified in heartache. But ask yourself what will you make of this pain? For your feeling of grief is simply the acknowledgment of your ability to love. I pray you find meaning in your suffering, like Papa.

WRITING EXERCISES

Grief, the response to loss, is an emotional process we all share. Take some time to write about your experiences with grief.

What did you learn? How did you grow?

_____

_____

_____

_____

_____

_____

_____

Were you able to find meaning in the grief?

_____

_____

_____

_____

_____

_____

Are there things that you learned from the process of grieving that influence how you might deal with loss in the future?

_____

_____

_____

_____

_____

_____

_____

_____

_____

BE READY

OCTOBER 25

Schuyler and I have been hitched at the hip for 32 years of otherworldly bliss, over three decades of polkadots and moonbeams. Do you want to know the secret? Sure, you do. Don't tell anyone but...

We have sex almost every day!

Almost on Monday. Almost on Tuesday...

[Insert ba-dum-dum-ching]

This flaccid dad joke was Wayne Dyer's opening line for years. He admittedly nicked it from nutrition pioneer Jack LaLanne, who opened the first fitness gym in Oakland, California in 1936. Hence, I feel absolved for pilfering it here.

Wayne was my first spiritual teacher. I met him once backstage when he lectured at Wanderlust in Lake Tahoe. After a frivolous chat about how nothing real ever changes, he reached out with his warm catcher's mitt of a hand and said, "Jeff, stay close to the work. And be ready."

There's hard evidence that Schuyler and I exceeded the "almost" at least three times. Schuyler, who was herself born at home, never questioned where she wanted to birth our babies. We attended (i.e. she dragged me to) a workshop in lower Manhattan led by Ina May Gaskin, the legendary author and midwife. Gaskin has delivered hundreds of babies at her midwifery clinic on The Farm, an intentional community located in Summertown, Tennessee. Gaskin was a pioneer in re-envisioning birth as a natural process (or, the most natural process of all) and cataloged the litany of medical interventions that can lead to complications in the hospital. Home birth is certainly not for everyone, but, for better and for worse, Schuyler, like you, is not everyone.

As a homebody, I was quite content to follow Schuyler's lead. Remaining snug in your jammies, avoiding the hailing of cabs mid-contraction, steeping rooibos in your own teapot. Comforts like these that breed serenity and minimize stress are friends of childbirth.

Our eldest daughter, Phoebe, was born in the guest room of her great-grandfather's house on the Connecticut shore. Like the cocktails, the day was dark and stormy. The grandparents numbed their imaginations with Meyer's rum as Schuyler raucously labored in the adjoining room. After our little Leo emerged, the blue fish started jumping and a rainbow arced over Long Island Sound. I'm not lying.

The setting for the nativity of number two was considerably less bucolic. Ondine was born in a basement in Brooklyn. It wasn't a dank, cement, bare-bulb type of cellar, but it wasn't exactly Gatsby either.

We found a midwife named Cara who lived on the Lower East Side. It wasn't far from our Williamsburg apartment as the crow – or, in this case, the stork – flies but it was a bit of a schlep on the subway. Cara was a former fashion model and her office was riddled with dozens of framed photos of her former fabulousness. I found this distracting. Nevertheless, we felt quite confident in Cara's custody and, together, we hatched our birth plan.

The doting husband assumes significant admin in a home birth. I'm not complaining. Despite the transformational experience women have as portals for new life, I wouldn't swap roles for all the tea in China. I doubt I could be so brave. Dutifully, I ordered the receiving blankets and drop cloths, the peroxide and the sponges. I froze the sanitary pads with dabs of witch hazel tincture. I rented the six-foot inflatable tub and jiggered a makeshift hose from the laundry room to fill it. I carried endless cauldrons of boiling water down the narrow stairwell to keep the tub at a balmy temperature.

At game time, the primary expectation was that I win the Emmy for best supporting role in a drama. To fully be there—emotionally and physically. And ...to bravely wield the mighty mini-strainer just in case any pushes yield buoyant brown nuggets in the tub. I didn't fancy this function so much.

Our due date was in June. Coincidentally, Ricki Lake released her brilliant documentary on home birth, "The Business of Being Born" at the Tribeca Film Festival in May. Cara was heavily featured in the film and reveled in the limelight of it all. I suppose we felt vaguely notable by association but Cara, reliving her erstwhile stardom, became less accessible. It didn't really concern us. We were veterans. We'd been through this before.

The morning arrived, Saturday, June 23rd. We were patient patients. When the contractions were consistently two minutes apart, I rang

Cara. She'd be right over. I helped Schuyler down the stairs into the cellar. We had a big blue yoga ball, an inversion swing, a quasi-dance bar you could hang on, and, of course, the ersatz jacuzzi. It was like a mini birthing Olympics.

Our doula, Tanya, arrived, thankfully, with bagels. My mum whisked Phoebe off to the Coney Island Mermaid Parade. Schuyler's mother and I balanced each other on a teeter-totter of nerves, busying ourselves. When in doubt, boil water. And Schuyler, bless her soul, went to work.

Matters were progressing slowly like a low-scoring baseball game. At the top of the third inning, my phone chirped the opening riff of Ice Ice Baby, my ringtone for Cara. I picked up and she literally said, "Are you sitting down?"

Cara wasn't coming. She had another client in Queens who had gone into labor a month early and Cara felt, rightfully, that her situation was more pressing than ours. Few instances in life have ever tested my threshold of compassion like this call. As cortisol flooded the highways of my veins, my reptilian brain inwardly screamed, "What about my fucking wife!" Instead, I shakily scribbled down the number of Cara's back-up, Miriam, and hung up.

I briefly debated whether or not I should tell Schuyler that her midwife was headed to another borough, as if eventually she might not notice. This reticence might reflect my ludicrous approach to psychological problem solving: sweep it under the rug and hope it will disappear. But, as casually as I could muster, I tossed the news down the stairs like a gently pitched cornhole beanbag.

Schuyler, well in the throes of it now, emphatically roared back, "I don't give a shit."

Next, I dialed Miriam who picked up on a scratchy line. I briefly painted the scene. She was chill and asked for directions. In return, I solicited her whereabouts. She was in a car headed north on I-87 near Woodstock. For those of you not familiar with the geography of the Northeast, that is bloody far away from Brooklyn! Two hours on the very best of days.

Reality crashed over me and pinned me momentarily to the seafloor. As I surfaced, a steely resolve set in. I was going to deliver this baby.

I suppose I could have rummaged through YouTube. Typing "how to deliver a baby" in the search box may scream of absurdity but, lo and behold, the platform is flush with turbaned hippies providing guidance.

Instead, I calmly took off my clothes and got in the tub with her. I don't remember much of the next ninety minutes, just that evolutionary biology unwound. We became animals, moaning together, our intuition pulling us inexorably forward. Schuyler was stunning, pushing with controlled ferocity and returning to the breath.

And, finally, Schuyler pierced me with her eyes and uttered, "I can't do this." Of course, this meant that she was on the precipice of delivery. I cautiously slipped my hand between her legs and felt our baby crowning. I must admit there was a tiny part of me that wanted to push that diminutive cranium back up the birth canal. But, instead, we braced for the next push and ...

Ding dong.

Really? A commercial break with 5 seconds left in the game.

Did I actually say "wait right here?" I don't recall. I trundled up the stairs like a wet retriever and swung the door open. There was Miriam. Somehow, she knew exactly where to go. I trailed her, already loyal.

She flipped open a mini-valise of miscellany; a handheld Doppler, a fetoscope, clamped scissors to cut the umbilical cord, Vitamin K and a set of sterile gloves. She motioned to me to kneel behind Schuyler with my biceps underneath her armpits. She stepped into the tub, squatted down and felt around. So fluent were her hands that she looked calmly up at the ceiling as she surveyed. And then, with a tender effortlessness, caught Ondine, our little wave, and placed her gently on my beloved's chest.

A profound silence impregnated the room, the permeating hush of gratitude, the acknowledgment of the astonishing miracle of life. So transcendent was this moment of utter presence that quite astoundingly, Schuyler, drunk with oxytocin, looked up at me and said, "Let's have another."

And we did.

Miriam delivered our third daughter as well; in the same cellar, in the same tub, with the same confidence and grace. We were humble in the preparations for Micah's birth. We took the time to actually meet the back-up, just in case.

Ondine's birth story was a reminder of the certainty of uncertainty. Despite the best-laid plans of mice and men, life is unpredictable, anything can happen.

Uncertainty is the nemesis of the conceptual mind. We seek control through knowing and, in the presence of unpredictability, it is too easy to succumb to fear. Our ability to reason, discern and act ethically is debilitated in this state.

Why do we meditate, practice yoga, breathe and sit in silence? There are myriad reasons, one of which is to be able to witness fear and not become it, to understand it as a transitory phenomenon passing through your consciousness moment by moment.

Viktor Frankl wrote, "Between stimulus and response there is a space. In that space is our power to choose our response. In our response lies our growth and our freedom." We practice to cultivate this sacred space within us.

Over the course of our personhood, the unexpected will inevitably rear its head time and again. The unforeseeable colors not only our personal lives – our babies and relationships, jobs and projects – but also our global humanity. We are living in a time punctuated by uncertainty. It is increasingly difficult to distinguish between fact and fiction. We are careening toward an election the outcome of which may not be revealed for some time. The institutions that have long provided stability are showing fissures of fragility.

A new, somewhat confounding reality is being birthed and the midwife may not show. But we must not accede to fear. We must commit to our daily practice such that we create the space between stimulus and response. This space will guide us toward right work and right action.

Let me whisper to you the words of a wise man, "Stay close to the work. And be ready."

Uncertainty will make its way into everyone's life at some point, and many fight against it tooth and nail. Reflect upon your own need for certainty in your life. Which aspects of uncertainty make you uncomfortable? Why?

Write about a time when things did not go as planned. How did you react?

_____

_____

_____

_____

_____

_____

_____

_____

_____

_____

_____

_____

Write about a time when you were able to find the space between an event and your reaction to it?

_____

_____

_____

_____

_____

_____

_____

_____

_____

_____

_____

_____

_____

_____

A SOLEMN PLEDGE

NOVEMBER 1

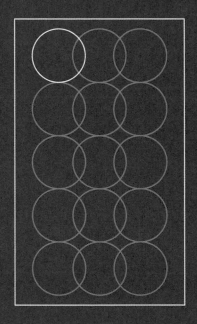

As the 2020 election race between the Democratic candidate, former Vice President Joe Biden, and the incumbent, President Donald Trump, neared, voter-fraud related rumors were rampant on social media and mistrust in the election process was at an all-time high. In the weeks prior to the election, there was record turnout in early voting states. By election day, more than 100 million Americans had voted early–either in person or by mail in ballot. Social media giants tried to combat misinformation online with fact checkers, an experiment with mixed results. COVID-19 hospitalizations had spiked by an estimated 46% from the previous month, and the country surpassed more than 9 million coronavirus cases, along with the highest death count globally. An mRNA vaccine was in phase three trials, and the first drug to treat COVID-19, Remdesivir, was approved by the FDA.

In 1987, I ran for high school president. It was a hotly contested race with many worthy candidates. I ran on a populist, if flimsy, platform of pizza Fridays and Van Halen on the snack bar jukebox. My campaign relied heavily on superlative slogans: Krasno Knows, JPK All the Way, It's About Jeffin' Time. And we made appeals to foreign-language speakers with Jeff Pour Le Chef and Jefe Por El Jefe. I glad-handed the beefcakes and lugged the girls' textbooks to class. I affixed placards to the sign-posts and stuffed lockers with handbills. I suffered through supplemental chapel sessions to underscore my scrupulous moral character. Had there been babies, I would have kissed them, a strategy I assiduously refused to deploy with the cheerleaders. I went careening into election day brimming with confidence.

The poll results were typed on a notecard and tacked to the student bulletin board the next morning. People crowded around the notice like locusts, a gossipy buzz permeating the halls. I elbowed my way to the front and my heart sank like a sack of sand. Amanda Tuttle, the spunky blond lacrosse player with the ski jump nose, would be the president. Finishing second, I would fulfill the drab ceremonial burdens of Vice President, which largely consisted of wretched flag duty. Stunned, I searched for answers. Maybe it was the fake dossier alleging lurid entanglements with my Russian teacher? Maybe I shouldn't have joined the Adrenochrome Club?

Rejected and dejected, I moped off to English Lit, *Death of a Salesman* in hand.

My English teacher, Blair Torrey, was a tree-trunk of a man, short and stocky yet full of vigor. He embodied every facet of the Renaissance man; a skilled sportsman schooled in the classics of Latin and Greek, able to quote Burns and Eliot at the drop of a Tudor flat cap. His keen emotional intelligence picked up on my dolefulness, as I slumped into my chair like Willie Loman.

"Mr. Krasno," he barked, "What is the etymology of the word 'vote'?"

Bothered and bewildered, I shrugged.

The fight to deny and abridge these rights has been leveraged with equal passion. Almost as fast as rights were won, barriers were erected to undermine the enfranchisement of minority groups: Religious requirements, property qualifications, poll taxes, and literacy tests. The powerful, left and right, employ a sinister dexterity in their quest to preserve their toehold on sovereignty.

And then, in an act right out of Dead Poet's Society, Torrey scooped up a weighty and frayed antediluvian Webster's dictionary and hurled it at me from across the room. Like a fat tuna, it landed with a sonorous thud on my desk. He peered over his spectacles, the edges of eyes tightening, spurring me along.

I flipped through the timeworn yellowed pages until I found the entry. I knew better than to simply recite the definition, so I skipped to the derivation.

The word "vote" is derived from the Latin votum "a vow, wish, promise to a god, dedication, a solemn pledge."

"Krasno, you weren't running for school president." Torrey loved the pregnant pause, cueing up a statement of great gravitas. "You were asking for the solemn pledge of your classmates."

It's quite difficult to remember amidst the mud-slinging morass of our current political bog that there is anything remotely solemn or spiritual afoot. This spectacular rite of self-determination has been tainted to resemble an all-day slog at the DMV.

But, of course, many of history's most revered spiritual icons were engaged in profoundly political acts. Moses led the Israelites out of slavery in Egypt. Jesus was crucified for fighting against the exploitation of the poor and meek. Jeanne D'Arc was martyred at 19 for crusading against English domination. Gandhi, armed with the unassailable moral integrity of ahimsa, marched for Indian independence. Reverend King and many others including John Lewis and Ralph Abernathy prayed with their feet in the quest for racial equity. These heroes, and scores of others, dedicated their lives to giving a voice to the voiceless.

But our human narrative is also rife with countless examples of miscreant leaders, some of them history's darlings, steadfast to keeping the powerless in their place. Our American story is certainly no exception, from conception onward.

From the mid 17th-century and for a hundred years after, suffrage in the American colonies was restricted to white, male, Christian property owners. The United States Constitution, ratified in 1787, did not define voter eligibility, allowing each state to determine its own regulations. And, sluggishly, bit by painstaking bit, for nearly 250 years, we have inched along the arc of the moral universe to extend the franchise. The expansion of voting rights can be principally attributed to the courageous battles waged by passionate citizens generation after generation including the aforementioned civil rights champions as well as Susan B. Anthony, Elizabeth Cady Stanton, Alice Paul, Lucy Stone and Ida B. Wells.

In fact, the sacredness of this right can be judged by the measure of the sacrifice made by others to secure it.

No less than four of the fifteen post-Civil War constitutional amendments have been ratified to extend suffrage to various groups of disenfranchised citizens. The 15th Amendment (1870) prohibited the denial of voting rights based upon "race, color or previous condition of servitude." Women's suffrage was codified by the 19th Amendment (1920). The 24th Amendment (1964) illegalized the poll tax. And the 26th Amendment (1971) established the national minimum age standard of eighteen.

The fight to deny and abridge these rights has been leveraged with equal passion. Almost as fast as rights were won, barriers were erected to undermine the enfranchisement of minority groups: Religious requirements, property qualifications, poll taxes, and literacy tests. The powerful, left and right, employ a sinister dexterity in their quest to preserve their toehold on sovereignty.

This dark treachery of American history continues to haunt us today in a number of states, including the battleground of Florida. For years, convicted felons were denied the right to vote in the Sunshine state. In a 2018 referendum, Florida voters overwhelmingly approved a measure to restore the franchise to those with felony convictions who have served their sentences, as long as the crime committed was not murder or sexual abuse. This initiative added an astounding 1.4 million voters to the rolls. However, this year an appeals court deemed that the governor and legislature could impose a ruling that made felons ineligible unless they paid back all their outstanding court fines and fees. Of course, many are, understandably, unable to afford it. Thus, the battle rages on.

If you ever feel that your vote is inconsequential then ask yourself why the denial of that right is the wicked project of so many.

Once you have embraced the imperative of exercising your civic duty, take a step further. Ask yourself how you might shift the narrative of voting from a political salvo, discharged once every few years, to a deeper commitment, practiced daily.

This ritual of election is not merely transactional but, on an individual level, a spiritual expression. The right to pull a lever does not just register an assent for a candidate or proposition but is itself tethered to the heartstrings of your most profound moral convictions. Your vote is a wish to instantiate a world in greater alignment with your highest principles. And a vow to preserve the rights previously and often arduously gained.

Most of us subscribe to the universal spiritual and moral principles of love and empathy. And these precepts may foster, in our mind's eye, a vision of a world that is more just and equitable, more harmonious and sustainable. Our vote is the distillation, if an imperfect one, of this imagined world our hearts know is possible. Such an understanding of this civic exercise may serve as a potent lens through which to contemplate to whom and what we offer our solemn pledge.

We cast our vote for people and ideas in the form of leaders and policies on federal, state and local levels. If we embrace this rite as not just a civic duty but also as an expression of our highest self, what are the traits and attributes we seek in our presidents and congress people, in our bills and propositions?

Very often, our civic mindedness is galvanized by what we are against. But it is ultimately far more sustainable to be mobilized by what we are for. In superlative leadership, the body politic thirsts for the elixir of wisdom and compassion.

Wisdom emerges from a critical study of one's own experiences, particularly one's failures. It is reflected in sound judgment and discernment. It is characterized by contemplative, unbiased and decisive responsiveness to situations, not impulsive reactivity.

Wisdom can be considered a moral quality, both separate and connected to knowledge. The French Renaissance philosopher, Michel de Montaigne wrote, "We can be knowledgeable with other men's knowledge but we cannot be wise with other men's wisdom." Sapient leadership is not boastful nor does it not revel in the accumulation of facts and figures. Instead, it cultivates an awareness of what it does not know. The wisest leaders surround themselves with others who have capacities and talents that infill the empty caves of inadequacy. Great leadership recognizes its own deficiencies and opportunities for growth. In this way, wisdom and humility are interwoven. Consider these sage writings on leadership from Lao Tzu, the father of Taoism:

A great nation is like a great man:
When he makes a mistake, he realizes it.
Having realized it, he admits it.
Having admitted it, he corrects it.
He considers those who point out his faults as his
most benevolent teachers.
He thinks of his enemy as the shadow that he himself casts.

And:

All streams flow to the sea because it is lower than they are.
Humility gives it its power.
If you want to govern the people, you must place yourself below them.
If you want to lead the people, you must learn how to follow them.

That these quotations are as prescient today as they were 2,500 years ago, during the time of the warring states, illustrate simultaneously their perennial truthfulness and humanity's staggeringly protracted moral evolution.

Great leadership must also embody compassion: lovingkindness in the presence of suffering. Through an empathetic emotional connection to others, the eminent leader inhabits a psychological state predisposed to alleviating another's suffering.

Compassionate leadership also seeks to empower and encourage others, decentralizing decision-making through distributed leadership. It seeks not credit but accepts responsibility. Here, again, are the wise musings of Lao Tzu from the 17th verse of the Tao Te Ching:

The best leaders are those their people hardly know exist.
The next best is a leader who is loved and praised.
Next comes the one who is feared.
The worst one is the leader that is despised.
The best leaders value their words, and use them sparingly.
When they have accomplished their task,
the people say, "Amazing! We did it, all by ourselves!"

The specific policies championed by consummate leadership are too many and diverse to enumerate in a measly weekend newsletter. However, as we peer inward to determine the initiatives we will support and oppose, we would do well to understand them inside these parentheses: Does the policy minimize suffering and maximize well-being for as many people as possible?

The diminishment of suffering and the maximization of human well-being can be mapped onto policies that help us either survive or thrive, that protect us or foster prosperity.

If government were to fulfill a hierarchy of needs, the wide foundation of the political pyramid would be the task of keeping citizens safe. Humanity currently faces myriad existential threats, and a willingness and ability to understand the complex, shifting nature of these menaces is of paramount importance in our prospective leaders.

Misinformation is more likely to be weaponized in the 21st century than green men on a battlefield. The impending infocalypse may deep fake us into further social incoherence. When fact and fiction become utterly indistinguishable, our ability to cooperate in the projects of humanity will shatter into a million of shards of fragmented reality.

We are capable of creating an S&P 500 of happiness and human fulfillment based upon a combination of these measurements: Life expectancy, homelessness, literacy and education levels, peace, child poverty statistics, renewable energy usage, ocean and forest sustainability, rates of incarceration, wealth distribution, sane drug policy, comprehensive treatment of chronic disease and mental illness, social cohesion, and public good will and trust.

Climate cancer, as Simon Sinek aptly dubs it, is threatening our coastlines, intensifying weather events, acidifying our oceans, reducing biodiversity, reducing our agricultural land to desert, and spawning millions of environmental refugees.

While food scarcity looms on the horizon, obesity and associated chronic disease may be as perilous in some parts of the world as famine is in others.

Of course, there is a biological pathogen to reckon with and learn from. As destructive as the current one is, the fatality rate of the next one may be twenty-fold.

These hazards, among others, will only further stress the centuries old project for racial equity that still cries out for criminal justice reform and equal access to housing, education and economic advancement.

As a bulwark against these shape-shifting menaces and challenges, we need leadership committed to sound and comprehensive technological, environmental, public health and social justice policy.

Beyond protecting our ability to survive, we seek policy that helps us thrive.

We look for innovative approaches to spur economic vitality while also protecting our most vulnerable from the sharper edges of capitalism.

Gross domestic product per capita can surely be a metric to measure our fiscal vibrancy. But, increasingly, we need to develop other metrics that more accurately depict our societal well-being beyond the Dow Jones Industrial Average.

We are capable of creating an S&P 500 of happiness and human fulfillment based upon a combination of these measurements: Life expectancy, homelessness, literacy and education levels, peace, child poverty statistics, renewable energy usage, ocean and forest sustainability, rates of incarceration, wealth distribution, sane drug policy, comprehensive treatment of chronic disease and mental illness, social cohesion, and public good will and trust.

If well-being is a shared goal, then the policies we support must ladder into these metrics.

The problems confronting us are immense, and you may feel at times paralyzed or numb in the face of them. But the world is not something happening to you. You are an active part of it. The human condition is merely the aggregate of billions of little decisions. Your vote is a recognition of self as a mere modification of a greater consciousness.

When you go to yoga class or sit in meditation, you may have an intention for that practice. Perhaps you vow to send lovingkindness to a friend in need or forgive someone who has done you wrong. Maybe you simply want to cultivate mindfulness, to sit in a non-judgmental awareness of the present moment. No matter your purpose, when the practice finishes, the intention does not simply disappear. In fact, in many instances, that intention is further fortified.

The same is true when exercising your right to vote. You will certainly have an intention with your vote. However, when the practice of voting concludes and the returns are tabulated, this intention does not evaporate. Maybe your candidate wins, maybe not. But your vote is merely a snapshot of a life's journey. An election will surely have substantial consequences. It will set the ranks for a period. But your right work and right action will endure and persist.

Take your vow, express your voice, make your solemn pledge. Rejoice and cheer, bellow and cry. And get back to work. The world needs you.

What are the qualities you look for in a leader?

What are the policies that are most important to you?

_____

_____

_____

_____

_____

_____

_____

_____

_____

_____

_____

How do your policy positions reflect your moral and/or spiritual convictions?

_____

_____

_____

_____

_____

_____

_____

_____

_____

_____

_____

_____

_____

_____

COMMUNION

NOVEMBER 8

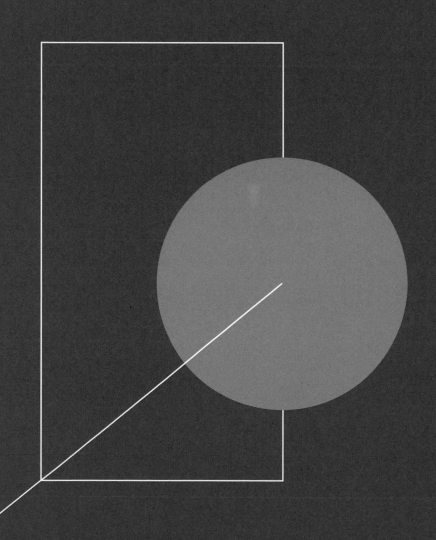

I grew up without much religion. I briefly attended the Unitarian Church as a result of a negotiation between my parents to placate their respective families. My mother was raised Methodist from strong Midwestern stock. My father is Jewish, and is bald, fancies rye bread and lives in Southern Florida if you need further proof.

I remember the Unitarian Church as a feel-good operation, a bit like a field day where all the kids got ribbons even when finishing last. I resonated with the minimal dogmatism and absence of a monopolistic claim to theological truth. The Unitarians essentially portrayed Jesus as a nice Jewish boy and the exemplar model for living one's own life, not as the earthly incarnate of an invisible creator of the universe.

I currently fashion myself as Buddhish, spiritually Buddhist and culturally Jewish. As a kid though, while I wasn't a heathen, I wasn't exactly walking in the footsteps of the ascendant host either.

When I was ten and living in Connecticut, I had a best friend named Patrick Murphy. You could live within the walls of the Vatican and not be as Catholic as Patrick's family. Patrick and I would engineer sleepovers every weekend, eat popcorn into the wee hours and relentlessly watch Grease on VHS, rewinding the bit with Olivia Newton-John dancing on the Shake Shack in her tight leather pantaloons. That was my conception of heaven. To this day, I hold a petty resentment that Patrick always assumed the role of Danny Zuko in our imaginary Fairfield County gang life. I was left playing the unsavory and morally rudderless Kenickie.

One Sunday morning in January, we woke to a foot of snowy powder. In what might be considered divine intervention, my parents were unable to fetch me from the Murphy's. Our impious driveway was snowed in.

"No worries," replied Mother Murphy, with a Christian sunniness that belied the weather. "We'll bring Jeffrey to mass with us." A nauseating dread consumed me as I eavesdropped the call. I had barely set foot in a church, let alone attended a formal mass.

Even though the sleeves ended halfway up my forearms, I packed my corpulence into Patrick's slim-fit blazer in much the same way that we crammed into Murphy's minivan. Evidently, their drive had magically been plowed by a celestial seraphim overnight.

We disembarked at St. Aloysius, the Catholic parish in town, and waddled single file into the church, the upstanding parents leading the way and children dutifully following; Kevin, Megan, Erin, Colleen, Patrick and me, bringing up the rear.

Thankfully, this waterfowl sequence landed me on the end of the last row of pews, my natural habitat. I have always associated my proclivities for anxiety, hypochondria and claustrophobia with my Jewish heritage. Somewhere buried in Leviticus it is likely decreed that those who escapeth enslavement from Egypt must sit on the aisle, else they panic convinced they're having cardiac arrest.

Adorned in a resplendent bejeweled frock, the priest strolled majestically to the altar. The congregation crossed themselves and settled. Befuddled, as if I were in an ASL crash course, I mimicked awkwardly the best I could and sat down. The priest's sermon drew from the Book of John. It was the story of an adulteress who had been brought to Jesus for condemnation by a group of men keen to stone her. Jesus demurred a reply but the men kept demanding an answer, so Jesus stood up and said, "All right, but let the one who has never sinned cast the first stone." The men sheepishly left and Jesus forgave the woman and told her to sin no more.

As the liturgy came to end, the congregation stood and people began to file down the nave toward the altar. Everyone began to sing a hymn. I recognized all sorts of folks from my town. My friends, Brian and Peter, from my basketball team, with their families. The Riggio's who ran the eponymous pizza parlor downtown. Manuel, the crossing guard from South School. And Mr. C, my math teacher, who wore cardigans and overused Binaca spray.

Patrick whispered to me to follow him down the nave to take Holy Communion. Petrified, I floundered down aisle, hands clenched in prayer, trudging toward the unknown. I reached the front, and shakily formed a throne with my hands. The priest intoned something incomprehensible in Latin and placed a wafer in my sweaty cupped palms.

As a boy with significant appetite, I was mildly disappointed in the measly, singular cracker with a cross on it. It wasn't until I was outside that I was informed that I had partaken in the body of Christ himself, if perhaps only a sacred hangnail.

The congregation had thronged to the plaza outside the parish, solemnity giving way to an equally fervent jocular camaraderie. Folks back-slapped and laughed, exchanged compliments and admired each other's children. For this ephemeral moment, on this picturesque snowy day, roles and rank dissolved. A group of people of diverse race, creed and political persuasion congregated to acknowledge something bigger than themselves. And, in the receipt of this Holy Eucharist, in the utter humility of it, a communion of souls extended beyond the walls of the church and the notion of a separate self briefly vanished.

The monumental election of 2020 is mercifully over and the winner is determined. Some will cry tears of joy and jubilation and others of sorrow and indignation. But after a year of indelible anguish and vitriol, a catharsis is overflowing into the streets, like champagne spouting from a shaken bottle. We can hear a giant exhale, a collective purification of spirit and purgation of fear. To watch my three daughters intently transfix their eyes to the Vice President-Elect, as she delivers her speech, restores my hope in American possibility.

The outcome is tremendously meaningful, particularly for those who have been impacted by the policies of the past 4 years, but the ground conditions in our country remain the same. While a new president will take the highest oath, if Americans are going to confront the colossal challenges ahead, each one of us must commit to the sacred oath of the citizen. We will need to find common ground. Even more, we will need to recognize our common humanity, to appreciate that, behind the plate mail armor of our political selves, we share the sorrows of death, the joys of new life, the trials of work, the thrills of accomplishment and the hopes for a better world for our children.

E Pluribus Unum, "Out of Many, One," is the long-standing motto of the United States approved by Congress in 1782. This maxim speaks to a shared recognition that, as individual citizens, we collectively participate in the greater national project for freedom and justice. That our liberation is indeed bound. However, as I sit here typing, there is little sense of unity or oneness in our nation. The cultural chasm that gapes

There is real hurt in these communities, places that once thrived with manufacturing jobs and vibrant downtowns, now moonscapes pocked with mini-marts, boarded up retail and fentanyl. These communities, mired in economic despair, long neglected and flown over, find agency in this President. And in this agency, life has meaning where it might otherwise not. This is potent. We all want to be heard and seen.

between Americans has never been wider or deeper. We are bunkered in tribes of political identity, tethered by our ankles to the thoroughbred of social media dreck that gallops toward one extreme or another dragging us along, leaving our nation drawn and quartered.

Given the freshness of the wounds, it will take considerable time for our cultural lacerations to scab and heal, but the noble hearted among us must begin to suture the gash. This is my purpose here, both at Commune and in my broader life, to foster community through compassion and conversation, to create a safe and inclusive space in which people can disagree without being disagreeable. I believe in true belonging, being accepted without compromising your beliefs, and tolerance for everything except intolerance.

The following observations are just my own and I am quite certain that your input will only improve them. This is the nature of ideas. In an open marketplace, the best notions simmer, commingle and bubble to the surface.

I did not choose our out-going President. I find him to be a confection of vice and believe his pathological narcissism and mendacity are a political danger. But these sentiments do not extend de facto to those who support him. In response to those on the left who seem incredulous as to how any sane human could endorse this President, I have worked hard to understand his appeal and his utility. And over the past months, through extensive communication, I have made efforts to cultivate relationships with his supporters. In order to work together, we need to understand each other.

He has become a champion for the white working class, largely left in the dust of corporate globalism. There is real hurt in these communities, places that once thrived with manufacturing jobs and vibrant downtowns, now moonscapes pocked with mini-marts, boarded up retail and fentanyl. These communities, mired in economic despair, long neglected and flown over, find agency in this President. And in this agency, life has meaning where it might otherwise not. This is potent. We all want to be heard and seen.

When I listen, really intently listen, to rural voters – like Susan, from Susquehanna County, Pennsylvania, who has become a regular presence in my Sunday inbox – what I hear is a deep resentment of being shamed. They don't like being called racist and ignorant. Who would? These are the most profound insults one can levy and for good reason. This President does not pass judgment on these folks. And it might be argued that, through his own moral vacancy, he expiates their sins. A man who embraces the meek, passes no judgment and expiates sin. Does that remind you of someone?

It is said, "Wise are those who look at others with the same generosity they offer themselves, and at themselves with the same critical eye they have for others." Given that essentially 70 million people pledged for each candidate, more than in any either previous election, neither side can logically argue the other is completely deranged. In the pursuit of common ground, it may be time for both left and right to turn a critical eye on itself.

And here I will teeter on a tightrope spanned over the third rail. These are the hard, thorny conversations of reconciliation.

It must be our collective project to eradicate racism from every corner of the earth. The murder of George Floyd and the subsequent national reckoning for racial justice has inspired many to engage in a deep moral inventory, to examine their implicit biases and to question historical narratives. Personally, I can attest to having learned more in the last six months than I learned studying race relations in college about the war on drugs, criminal justice reform, the history of the American police, redlining and housing policy, and the scale of the persistent wealth gap.

But while the white left unpacks their complicity in systemic injustice and attempts to untangle the web of privilege, it also seems all too ready to sanctimoniously levy the epithet of "racist" on anyone who deviates from its orthodoxy.

My pen pal Susan is a white single mother living in a trailer who works two minimum wage jobs at Burger King and Home Depot. Does shaming her, not for any reprehensible action but simply for her politics, advance the cause of racial justice? Because, while she may benefit in some ways from the color of her skin, I guarantee she *feels* no privilege, nor does she feel a sense of guilt for the atrocities her great-grandfather may have committed. She is simply scraping by.

This practice of hurling slurs, largely behind the shield of an iPhone screen, is not only arrogant, it is also, evidently, not good political strategy. And it will never bring us together. If we are committed to healing our country, and there's every reason to be, then perhaps white liberals can consider this aforementioned quotation before casting invidious aspersions, "Let the one who has never sinned cast the first stone."

Instead of broadening the definition of racism in a manner that ostracizes half of the population, we can unite around the collective project for racial equity; ending the war on drugs, enacting criminal justice reform (which has bipartisan support), expanding access to education and health care and building affordable housing.

As I read Susan's emails and others who echo her antipathy for the moral posturing of the left, I attempt to don her emotional clothing by understanding her lived experience. And, like some kind of strange cultural interpreter, I try to explain to her the lived experience of others, particularly marginalized people, who not only feel a denial of opportunity but unsafe in their own country. One group's empowerment cannot come at the expense of another's. She seems to hear it.

America will need a truth and reconciliation process that can lead to dialogue at scale. The road to reparations must be paved with empathy rather than shame. And part of this exercise will include the establishment of a shared vernacular.

The chasms that divide us as a result of misinformation and fearmongering are daunting, but more intractable still are the wedge issues that spring from deeply held personal beliefs. But if we are to bridge the cultural divide, we must now step back from our political and religious identities in an effort to recognize the moral underpinnings of our different respective beliefs.

One of the most prominent themes in my exchanges with Susan is that she believes that the left are all "socialists." She hurls the rubric with reckless abandon. The right has weaponized a warped misunderstanding of socialism. In reality, there is no leftist platform in support of collective ownership of industry or nationalization of banks. There is no one arguing against free market capitalism. There are social programs that include social security, Medicare, Medicaid, farm subsidies, public education and many others. These programs exist to dull the knife point of capitalism, to protect the vulnerable. The extent to which this safety net should be cast should be the topic of vigorous debate in a democracy, but to misrepresent these programs, especially to some of the people who need them most, is a crass kind of political maneuvering.

The chasms that divide us as a result of misinformation and fearmongering are daunting, but more intractable still are the wedge issues that spring from deeply held personal beliefs. But if we are to bridge the cultural divide, we must now step back from our political and religious identities in an effort to recognize the moral underpinnings of our different respective beliefs.

I have written extensively about human moral intuition. Sitting behind religion, I believe there is an innate shared sense of universal truth. Before Moses raised a stone tablet above his head etched with "thou shalt not steal," we collectively knew thievery to be unethical. And this precept is virtually unanimous despite our religious affiliations.

I contend that a belief in a common moral bedrock can undergird our political and social identities as well.

For example, Susan considers her "pro-life" stance as a deeply moral one. There may be no issue more culturally divisive than abortion. Those who are "pro-life" castigate the other side as morally bereft in their disregard for the sanctity of human life. Those who are "pro-reproductive freedom" rage against their opponents for their disrespect of a woman's right to control her own body. You can set your watch to the party affiliations of these positions.

We can debate incessantly about whether life begins at conception, whether the government has a right to dictate a woman's decisions over her own body or why legal abortion is really just safe abortion. But is it possible to find a spirit that recognizes that the positions adopted by both sides are rooted in profound moral conviction? And though legal wrangling will always be fractious, is there not at least the possibility of uniting around a shared goal of minimizing abortion through supporting women, addressing the root causes of unwanted pregnancies and providing wide access to family planning?

The rancor of this time has not only worn the nation threadbare, but it has ruptured friendships and torn families apart. If there is any remote hope of finding reconciliation, we must collectively eschew our addiction to social media. The weaponization of misinformation on Facebook, Twitter, and YouTube imperceptibly pushes us toward the edges, radicalizes our opinions and lures us into acts of public vitriol, executed in private. Social media may be the primary engine of our national self-hatred. Healing will not happen digitally. It will only happen in real community. It will happen by powering down and going next door.

Four years ago, some felt emboldened in their beliefs by the outcome of an election. And, today, others feel a similar vindication. But I call on each of us to be brave enough to walk the middle path. This is not limp conciliation. On the contrary, the pursuit of unity emerges from a robust patriotism.

The first words enshrined in our greatest piece of American literature are *"We the people."* Compassion is brave. And it is compassion we must now find to revive the quest for a more perfect *union*, to provide for the *common* defense, to promote the *general* welfare for these *United* States of America. It's time to heal. As the President-Elect implored, "Let this grim era of demonization begin to end here and now."

Jesus' sacrament is not marble and brass, but bread and wine. We must now bake the bread in order to break it with each other. We must sit around the supper table and drink wine with each other, not to be further drunken in our opinions, but to foster fellowship through hard conversation. Now is the time to summon the better angels of our nature, to sit together in a Holy Communion each of our making, for the sake of our flawed, beautiful, messy, soulful country.

God bless you. And God bless the United States of America.

WRITING EXERCISES

Behind all of our religion and cultural influences, there is a moral intuition that instinctively shapes our ethics. Sit quietly and examine how your sense of morality has been shaped by the external world. Then tune in to your core moral intuition.

What are some primary moral intuitions that you possess?

Can we use some of our moral intuitions to find common ground with those with whom we disagree?

_____

_____

_____

_____

_____

_____

What are some of the questions that we can ask behind the arguments that divide us? For example, instead of arguing over immigration policy, ask why someone would choose to leave their country and family? Instead of engaging in a polarized debate over abortion, ask what are the conditions that would lead a woman to make the choice to willingly abort a fetus?

_____

_____

_____

_____

_____

_____

_____

_____

_____

_____

_____

_____

_____

_____

_____

Try to engage compassionately with people in a way that respects their moral convictions and ask the questions behind the argument.

Why is finding common ground important?

ENOUGH IS A FEAST
NOVEMBER 29

By the time this ink hits the press, I'll be 50. I am reveling in the denoue-ment of my fifth decade, sipping tequila (as an anti-inflammatory of course) and teasing my ancient beloved, Schuyler, who turned 50 in April. Shot glasses, limes, salt, and associated ribaldry just specks in the rearview mirror. Now, I drink for my health, just a thimble to help with digestion while I curl up with Thoreau in front of a crackling fire. Against my will, I am becoming my father. For me, a pleasant fate, if a bit sedentary.

Maybe like you, I had grandiose designs for 2020, with its notable birthdays and silver anniversary. Even my daughters convinced me that turning 16, 13 and 10 were of significance. But quite quickly, the chain came off our family plans for a bicycle trip through Italy. Instead, we Zoomed a lot, binged Queen's Gambit and played online chess. My plans for a musical extravaganza birthday bash turned into a solo gig of sappy jazz ballads. But, if this birthday, or this year, proved anything, it's that enough is a feast. We hiked and cooked, read and wrote, talked and walked. The imposed monasticism of this strange and twisted year, and particularly this season, focused our gaze onto the abundance of what we have, not the scarcity of what we lack.

I was born on Thanksgiving Day in 1970 at the University of Chicago's Lying Inn hospital. I grew up one of those pitied kids whose birthday overlaps with a holiday. Instead of bowling my mates and plotting schemes to nick those groovy shoes, I was at Nana's house wearing a collared shirt. My Papa's birthday coincided as well. And due to the confluence of happy observances, the entire family made the annual Turkey Day pilgrimage to South Florida. Like a Kumbh Mela for lapsed Jews — the frosted-haired great-aunts, the twins I could never tell apart, the vegan uncle who never wore underwear, the cousins that grew a foot every year — we all made the schlep.

My sweet Nana feverishly planned for it all year. And though she always assured me that I was the biggest turkey of them all (as she surrep-titiously slipped me a fiver), I learned quickly to share the spotlight.

In truth, she told us all the same thing. There is only one grandchild prodigy in the world and every Jewish grandmother has one, or, in our case, six. While I wallowed in this annual ritual of family dramedy, sun burns and too much noodle kugel, I am not sure I fully appreciated it. Until now.

Until now, as I stare at my own children sparring over Parcheesi, losing myself in them, trying to be present and also helplessly sensing it slip away. Too soon, they'll be wanderlusting off on global conquests and, worse, visiting their wretched in-laws for holidays. At bloody 50, I channel the grim resignation of every parent as we cry, "Don't they know God is right here, dammit!" If the young knew and the old could.

While 50 orbits around the sun is a formidable distance, I don't want to get too mawkish with the symbolism of it. I suppose there is a part of me that is infinite and ageless. The me who resides outside of space and time, location and form. The me unwitnessable by the limitations of my five senses and science's genius to enhance them. The me outside the physical plane and the world of the 10,000 things. The unmutable me.

I only glimpse my limitless self in the hush of solitude. Melville wrote, "the one and only voice of God is silence." Silence is a portal into elevated consciousness as it may be the only human experience that is infinite. It has no beginning nor end. It takes no form, nor can it be located. Sitting in silence opens the door to a world unbound by the vacillations of space and time, to things that never change. And, in this utter emptiness, the very idea of "me" dissolves. There is only the world, a single all-enveloping Self of which you and I are merely modifications. This emptiness barely musters a placid smile over a man turning fifty.

And while I gaze upon this everlasting sunset from time to time, I know I cannot exist completely untethered to my personhood, this clumsy human experience of eating and pooping between thoughts. Here, in dull care, I still must chop the wood and carry the water. This is our common project; to continually re-stitch these cleaved realities, alloying the work of our body-mind with the awareness of a higher consciousness.

As my trunk acquires rings, I am beginning contemplate my legacy, not out of vanity, nor in terms of an epitaph. I am pondering what about me lives on after the drummer hits the final crash cymbal? What is the song after the curtain drops on the performance? What is it about my life that will outlive my life?

I keep thinking, hoping, that perhaps there is a way to contribute to the body of human knowledge in such a manner that the experience of what it is like to be human is better. We may all share the goal that the ripple of our ephemeral existence may maximize the well-being and minimize the suffering of those who follow. Let this be our collective dharma.

The most tangible vessels to carry the products of my life posthumously forward are my children. They have no choice but to sit at the dinner table and listen to me prattle on. You can just delete me with a flippant key stroke, but perhaps you'll linger a moment. I have begun to harvest the contents of my scattershot experiences, the abject failures and modest breakthroughs, and synthesize them into pint-sized lessons. Here are some aphoristic musings about life, as I have begun to understand it, that, at 50, I am sharing with my children:

Gratitude is not simply a state of thankfulness. Gratitude is most truly expressed by the works and actions in which one engages that recognizes the miracle of life's gifts.

Great leadership articulates a vision, fosters fluency around it and distributes power. A great leader clearly elucidates the mission and its supporting values which provide the lens through which an empowered community can make decisions. The great leader needs superlative judgment but does not need to, nor should, make all the decisions. This model of centralized mission and decentralized decision-making fosters trust, empowerment and, inevitably, healthy growth.

Profound love is not a transitory emotion passing through consciousness moment by moment. Love is an essence that emerges from the absence of need and births the possibility for compassion, forgiveness and generosity.

Conversation may be the most powerful vehicle for manifesting the world our hearts know is possible. Conversation requires vulnerability which is synonymous with courage. It fosters a recognition of our common humanity which is, above all, what the world so desperately needs. In a thoughtful marketplace of ideas, the best ones will cream to the top.

Commitment is often misconstrued as limitation and framed within the parentheses of sacrifice, of what one must give up. However, the bedrock of unconditional love is the launchpad for madcap risks and the pursuit of uncertain dreams. In failure, there is the comfort of deep allegiance to break the fall. In this way, commitment is freedom.

Genuine Community fosters true belonging, an acceptance of its members without demand that they sacrifice who they authentically are. Community requires tolerance for everything except intolerance. Community thrives in safety, trust and continuity.

Compassion brings lovingkindness to the presence of suffering in a manner that seeks to alleviate suffering. Compassion differs from empathy, the donning of another's emotional clothing. It has an innately positive valence that is vibrant and effusive. The practice of compassion represents humanity in its highest form.

Forgiveness is not only an offering to someone else, but it is also a gift you give yourself. When you are holding the ember of vengeance, it is you that is getting burned. In forgiveness, you drop the ember, overcome resentment and purge your spirit. Forgiveness does not forsake justice. You can forgive and still hold your offender accountable. It first transpires in the head and then, slowly, in the heart. Forgiveness is the most difficult virtue to practice.

A life of Integrity is one in which you align your works and actions with your highest principles irrespective of external circumstances.

Now that I am on life's back nine, or more actuarially, in the tee box of the 13th hole, I am making some resolutions. Just for an ego boost, I'll start with one I can keep: no duck. I don't like consuming waterfowl so that's an easy win to get me some momentum out of the gates. No sugar. Man, that's hard but I'm going to try. Meditate every day if only for a minute. I can do that. Fearlessly engage in thorny conversations. Sure, but difficult because I fancy being liked. Be present with my family. And write a book (even if I need to publish it myself!). I know all these things would be good for me, but, of course, the gap between knowing and doing can be daunting to breech.

Wisdom may just be listening to your own advice.

CHRISTMESS

DECEMBER 25

'Twas early Christmas morning, 1983.
And nary a creature was stirring, not even me.

Of course, my brother and I had designs on waking with the rooster's crow, rowdily rouse our parents and attack the trove of presents that bulged under the tree, spilling out over the candy cane apron 'round it.

But the cock-a-doodle-doo came in the form of a volley of jagged barbs shooting like arrows up the stairs from the kitchen and into my bedroom. I sprang out of bed and fetched my brother from his bunk. We scurried to the top of the stairs and snuggled into each other three steps down. He was seven and his pajamas still had feet.

Our parents squabbled often and Eric and I took a strange, masochistic delight in listening to them bicker. One parent would grab the red cape and goad the other to charge. And, like spectators at a bullfight, we muttered a quiet "Ole" under our breath as they dodged one another. We furtively tabulated the piercing stabs until this one morning when my father said, "Well, if you're planning to leave in June anyway, you might as well leave now."

My stomach hurtled into my throat like someone punched me in the Adam's apple, like I'd swallowed a melon. And, in an instant, sitting on those stairs with my brother under my arm on that Christmas day, my new broken life flickered before me.

As it is with grief, I did not accept it. I vowed to fix things. I would leverage everything in my power, including my own sanity, to save their marriage. I would be my brother's keeper. I would punish my mother. I would be unborn to her. This dematriation became the shadowy sub-plot of my fraught adolescence.

Of course, none of it worked. And, finally, against my will, many years later, I collapsed in surrender. I resigned to wisdom.

I don't mean to throw a wet stocking on your holiday yule log. As you will see, this story is not even remotely woeful. My point is that the holiday season is emotionally messy for most of us.

This is true in any year, but Xmas 2020 may well be the burnt-out star precariously balanced atop a most crooked tree. The celebration of this time without the presence of family is profoundly melancholic for many and a substantial relief for others.

This season expects our joy and, in a desperate bid for good tidings, we swill the pints of Christmas cheer. The piped-in choruses of major-keyed carols backdrop a frenzy of gift-wrapping, potato-mashing and cider-spiking. But while the twinkling lights shine bright on the tree, the branches cast a shadow in which our merriment is muted by bittersweet introspection. If your soul is one with the spirit of the season, God bless you. But if sorrow cleaves your heart right now, then, please know, you are not alone in your aloneness.

I recall traveling to Japan in the early 2000's. Suspended above the entrance of a sprawling underground mall in Fukuoka was an over-sized Santa nailed to a giant cross. I'd never witnessed the cultural hegemony of the West translated in such a gruesome and hilarious fashion. As the initial amazement waned, this crucified Claus begged a question: How did we get here?

How did the celebration of the nativity of a prophet transform into a commodified free-for-all led by a bespectacled man with fur-cuffed trousers? Upon reflection, I couldn't really blame the hapless Japanese bloke in charge of environmental décor for his befuddlement. The confusing emotional tumult of the season is mirrored by an equally confounding tradition.

A lithe, sandaled man hailing from the warm climes of Nazareth is commemorated by a rotund grandfather sporting galoshes befitting the North Pole. The apostles have grown antlers and pull a sleigh laden with Playstations (I reckon Blitzen is Judas Iscariot). We once sanctified Mary's incomparable chastity, and, now, in honor of the birth of her son, I dutifully fulfill the wish list of my eldest daughter with make-up from Sephora. Why not Santa on a cross?

Generally uninspired by the Holy Mother, Schuyler, bless her, was a virgin until twenty. I devoted two years of unsullied chivalry to my noble pursuit of her. (And in my prime years I might add.) I dubbed her private area the Kingdom of God, for there was more chance of a camel passing through the eye of a needle than a rich man entering it (Mark

10:25 ;-). I won't claim that our daughters were conceived immaculately, but it was damn close.

I particularly empathize with poor Joseph. Imagine all the nappies he devotedly changed without even a proper shag let alone much paternal credit. Just as The Holy Spirit "overshadowed" Mary, Joseph lives in the shadow of God. Strange that a religion that gives its savior two dads also promotes the fatal public stoning of homosexuals (Leviticus 20:13).

Evidently, the emergence of Santa Claus as Christ's proxy is a product of syncretism evolving over millennia. Saint Nicholas of Myra was a 4th-century Greek Christian bishop famous for his generous gifts to the poor, in particular presenting three impoverished daughters of a pious Christian man with dowries so that they would avoid a life of prostitution.

Father Christmas dates back to 16th-century England during the reign of Henry VIII, when he was portrayed as a large man in scarlet robes lined with fur. He exemplified the spirit of good cheer at Christmas, bringing peace, joy, good food, wine and revelry. As England no longer kept the feast day of Saint Nicholas on December 6th, the Father Christmas celebration was moved to December 25th to coincide with Christmas Day. Essentially, the traditional celebrations of Old Saint Nick and Christmas were merged.

The modern visual of our jolly, red-hatted Santa is derived from the 1823 poem by Clement Clark Moore, *A Visit from St. Nicholas* (more commonly known as *The Night Before Christmas*). The political cartoonist, Thomas Nast, also played a significant role in crafting his image. Of course, good old American capitalism embellished our jovial gift-giver as well. Coca-Cola sweetened Claus' persona throughout the 20th century with advertisement campaigns.

For years, I eschewed the holiday, deriding its over-commercialization, perhaps a reflection of an evolving anti-materialism, or maybe just a half-hearted attempt to spiritually bypass my adolescent trauma. I still give December 25 a minor side-eye but the unbridled holiday spirit of my children has slowly humbled, if impoverished, me. My daughters are a stark reminder that my life isn't all about me. It's about me in connection with them, with you, and with the world.

The messiness of the holiday season brings life's contradictions into stark relief. We experience both the joy and discomfort of togetherness while balancing the serenity and loneliness of solitude. We express the immaterial emotions we hold for one another in the form of material gifts. We celebrate the birth of a new beginning while grieving the passage of those we have loved. In growing, we accept the imperfect perfection of life's incongruities.

I'll never be that guy in the Christmas card wearing the reindeer antlers with the sparkly-toothed family in matching Rudolph sweaters. Behind every photoshopped depiction of feigned perfection, there are a hundred broken hearts. Still, what was once a lump of coal, over time, became a diamond. Sure, I've spent plenty of fraught energy navigating Christmas calendars between my parents, divvying up time fairly like slices of pumpkin pie. But, in the end, my mother and father were the absolute best parents they knew how to be. My mother bequeathed me persistence and creativity. My father imparted the love of music and a custody of words. In the end, they were my greatest teachers. And, of course, together, they gave me this miracle that I call my life. My love for them transcends the familial. I revere them as people.

I reflect upon those years of teenage tribulation, of reckless wrath. I picked up an ember from the crackling fire. In my fury, I clenched it, waiting for the right moment to hurl it at my mother, to exact my revenge. All that time, it was me getting burned. When you are angry, YOU are the one that is angry. With the wisdom that time brings, I now recognize that I, myself, was the source of my own suffering. So often, it is this way. I don't blame the child on the stairs but the imagined future of suffering that flashed before me was a phantom of my own projection. I do not contend that loss is not painful, but as one spiritually grows, so does the ability to respond to the event instead of reacting hastily to the judgment of it.

After Jesus hung upon the cross for three hours, he summoned his final words, "Father, forgive them, for they do not know what they do." (Luke 23:34)

The greatest gift you can give, this season or any, is forgiveness. And this gift extends potently to yourself. I have long since forgiven my parents for their shortcomings. But it took considerably longer to forgive myself. Consider wrapping up this present with a ribbon and sending it off in a self-addressed envelope.

If you can practice forgiveness, compassion, and gratitude for the abundance of what fills your life, then you will be walking in the footsteps of the baby born on this day. You will be finding Christ in the mess. Watch then the angels appear into your life as they recognize themselves in you. This can make any holiday a merry one.

That's all I have to exclaim as I drive out of sight.
Happy Christmas to all, and to all a good night.

WRITING EXERCISES

To be human is to experience pain. Reflect on a traumatic event from your life
when you felt wronged. Write it down.

_____

_____

_____

_____

_____

_____

_____

_____

_____

_____

_____

_____

_____

_____

_____

_____

Have you been able to come to peace with it? If so, how?

_____

_____

_____

_____

_____

_____

_____

_____

Write about someone you have forgiven. What happened? How did you arrive at the place where you were able to forgive? What happened after you forgave?

WHEN LIGHTNING STRIKES
DECEMBER 31

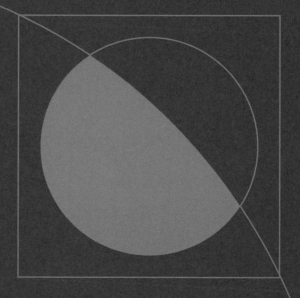

A hot white light encased me as a crystal vase shattered inside my head. Gone as fast as it came, this vivid encounter completely enveloped my entire being.

Last Sunday night, I lay in bed in the melancholic alpenglow of Christmas, knackered and bloated from holiday revelry. I was pondering the content of this very essay, mulling over resolutions, both personal and general, and their relationship to human potential. I was mentally dusting off my Maslow and his hierarchy of needs as rain began pattering like mice feet on the rooftop. Candidly, I felt a bit fallow, all my ideas harvested, milled, baked, sliced and served up. My mind cast about for droplets of inspiration to sponge up.

The drizzle had become a downpour. It hadn't rained but a spit since April in Los Angeles. Now, the heavens opened up. God's pent-up grief undammed in the waning verses of a most epic, if tragic, year. In the hot, dry climes of California, the first rains are an occasion for rejoicing. For years now, fire season has been merciless. This celebration, as you will read, was pre-mature.

Thunder echoed sonorously through the canyon. As a kid, I remember counting between the flashes of lightning and the ensuing rumblings, five seconds for a every mile. These lapses registered about a four and then a two.

And then, in a flick of a switch, Thor unleashed his fury and the world literally exploded around me. A massive bolt of lightning slapped our house with such intensity that it eclipsed all other discernible phenomena. It jolted us from bed. I patted myself down to make sure I was actually still corporally there. The kids, wide-eyed in shock, burst down the stairs. It was undoubtedly the most intense sensory experience I've ever had, the present moment in hyperbolized relief.

As the initial astonishment subsided, we huddled together in edgy laughter. And then the fire alarms began to sound. Almost indiscernible, serpentine streams of smoke slithered into the house. Schuyler and I corralled the children into the dry safety of the car and returned back inside. There were no obvious flames. We rummaged through the rooms trying to identify the elusive source.

The smoke thickened into a toxic haze that was acrid on the tongue. I darted into my closet and tossed my essentials into a backpack. I had never really considered what I'd jam into a small sack if that's all I had. Wallet, car keys, passport, cash, wedding ring, this laptop, the watch my dad gave me for graduating college – a sundry amalgam of my identity.

We scurried down the steps back toward the car. And, as we descended, the thought struck me like … The crawl space under the house! We crowbarred the small door open with our fingers and flames burst forth. To our great fortune, there was an impeccably positioned garden hose nearby. Schuyler grasped the nozzle and I ran to the spigot. In a few minutes the fire was doused. No sooner had we extinguished the fire than four massive engines from the LAFD barreled up the street sirens blaring. The gladiators disembarked laden with axes and fire hooks and finished the job.

Then the firemen left. And there we were: Schuyler, Phoebe, Lolli, Micah and me. 2am. Sopping wet from rain but without water. Adrenalized by a gigajoule of electricity yet without a working lamp. The twisted irony of fucking 2020, a year when even the rain brings fire.

I posted a little video on the affair. Honestly, I didn't think much of it. But, the next morning, I was humbled to read hundreds of beautiful comments from well-wishers, friends I hadn't heard from in years expressing relief that the family was safe. In particular I noticed a few supportive comments from people with whom I have vociferously quarreled on social media. My online squabbles, like most people's, tend to be political in nature. I always make best efforts not to be disagreeable in my disagreement. There's one fellow, let's call him Redpill Frank, who is constantly posting memes about the Kraken, Biden's pedophilia, how COVID is a hoax and on. He is particularly harsh on immigrants and was obsessed with the Soros-funded "caravan." I attempt to gently remind him that unless he is Native American or his family was brought to this country against their will then he also shares an immigrant story. I get nowhere and oftentimes it devolves. But, there he is, in my comments, sending me "best wishes." Somehow, lured outside the invective by the story of our misfortune, Frank found compassion.

Many people throughout history have considered lightning a divine and mystical event. I hate to discredit this myth, but, in reality, it resembles more of a fire in the cellar. There have been no celestial seraphim sightings. Instead, a multitude of pot-bellied, balding men with clipboards are parading onto our property, muttering things about the structural integrity of our house.

I suppose Maslow will have to wait. It's challenging for a man to self-actualize without running water. But it's not impossible to learn something.

In the deluge of contractors flooding my new year, I met Manuel. He's the young Oaxacan apprentice to our electrician, Juan. As Juan surveyed the fondue of wiring under the house, I made Spanglish small talk with Manuel. Evidently, when he came to America three years ago, he left behind his wife and young daughter, Ana, in Santa Catarina. He hasn't seen them in the flesh since. When I asked, he produced a photo of Ana – not a digital phantom on a screen, but a little 2" x 2" rough-edged snapshot that snuggled in his wallet. She's learning English, he told me. Manuel lives in Juan's garage, somewhere near Commerce to the east of downtown. The dubious structural integrity of my house in the canyon suddenly seemed less grave.

The polarized bickering between left and right on many topics, including immigration, is rarely a profitable project. The left indignantly refers to a statue in a harbor that brandishes an Emma Lazarus poem. It wields accusations of xenophobia. In turn, the right rails against the anarchic tendencies of the left, stereotyping immigrants as criminals, undermining our way of life and pilfering our jobs. This tete-a-tete ends inevitably in a cul-de-sac. I wonder if we might find the brave space behind the invidious barbs to ask the question: What are the ground conditions that exist that would compel Manuel to leave his country, his beloved family and his identity for a strange land with an unknown language that likely doesn't want him? I want to ask him this, but I have not the words.

The voltage struck the roof, assumedly the lightning rod, and traveled down through the wiring and copper pipes of the house seeking ground. In its quest, it blew the valves off the irrigation piping creating a series of non-decorative garden fountains shooting streams of water to and fro. This is proving to be quite a difficult project to repair. Sergio, bless his heart, is grappling with a plumber's version of whack-a-mole, in the dark, with a head lamp – just so my family can have water again. He is a portrait of diligence. In gratitude, Schuyler brings him tea.

After a laborious day of insurance claims and associated red tape, I thought of my political sniping partner, Frank. He's got a daughter, one that he sees every day. Maybe instead of sparring with him about immigration, I'll just relay the story of Manuel to him, not with the purpose of shaming him but, in the hopes that we may discover a shared humanity. This may point our dialogue toward solutions and away from rancor.

If we can warm our hearts in each other's human stories instead of codifying our positions like ice cubes in a tray, then perhaps we can melt into each other. By asking the question behind the argument, perhaps we can address the disease behind the symptom. Stories can be a lightning rod for connection. In each other's stories, we glimpse a bit of our own. And, in our shared fears of the uncertain, in our common joys, loves and worries, we are a little bit less alone.

You may be familiar with the old supernatural Hollywood motif: an otherwise normal protagonist gets struck by lightning and develops superpowers. I have received dozens of inquiries into the nature of my newly acquired capacities. I hate to disappoint but I remain unable to generate electrical energy and project it as concentrated bolts from my hands. But perhaps I can project a healing energy, in the form of stories, from my pen. My superpower, and yours, too, may be storytelling. And as I peer into a new year with its requisite resolutions, I am reminded that I don't need to manifest any *thing* into my life, I simply need to manifest who I already am – a teller of tales.

WRITING EXERCISES

Take a moment to reflect on a memorable story from your life and write it down.

Do you think other people can see their own story in yours? In what ways?

_____
_____
_____
_____
_____
_____
_____
_____
_____
_____

Does your story have any relevance to a prescient societal issue?

_____
_____
_____
_____
_____
_____
_____

What is your superpower?

_____
_____
_____
_____
_____
_____
_____
_____

Educational Resources on Race

Profound appreciation to Anasa Troutman for her personal generosity in organizing this list.

We must do all we can, every one of us, to instantiate a reality that extends all the protections and opportunities guaranteed in our mutual national contract to everyone. This must start with our selves, but also extend into every nook of humanity.

What can you do?
Honestly examine your implicit biases and change them. Read and educate yourself. See your personal wellness as inextricably tied with the well-being of society.

Listen
White Lies - NPR
www.npr.org/podcasts/510343/white-lies

The Big We Podcast
www.thebigwe.com/podcast

Seeing White – Scene on Radio
www.sceneonradio.org/seeing-white

Watch
Traces of the Trade – Katrina Browne
www.tracesofthetrade.org

King in the Wilderness – HBO
www.hbo.com/documentaries/king-in-the-wilderness

I Am Not Your Negro
www.iamnotyournegrofilm.com

The Wellness of We
www.thewellnessofwe.com

13th – Ava Duvernay / Netflix
www.netflix.com/title/80091741
www.youtube.com/watch?v=krfcq5pF8u8

Eyes on the Prize – PBS
www.pbs.org/wgbh/americanexperience/films/eyesontheprize

The Pieces I Am – Toni Morrison
www.tonimorrisonfilm.com

Read
Memphis Burning – Preston Lauterbach, Places Journal
https://placesjournal.org/article/memphis-burning

How To Be An Antiracist – Ibram X Kendi
www.ibramxkendi.com/how-to-be-an-antiracist

Me and White Supremacy – Layla F Saad
www.meandwhitesupremacybook.com

The Body is Not an Apology – Sonya Renee Taylor
www.thebodyisnotanapology.com/shop/uncategorized/
hard-copy-the-body-is-not-an-apology-the-power-of-radical-self-love

Between the World and Me – Ta-Nehisi Coates
www.penguinrandomhouse.com/books/220290/
between-the-world-and-me-by-ta-nehisi-coates

A Timeline of Events That Led to the 2020 'Fed-Up'-rising –
Michael Harriot, The Root
www.theroot.com/a-timeline-of-events-that-led-to-the-2020-fed-up-
rising-1843780800

INDEX

1. charleseisenstein.org/essays/the-coronation/

2. www.history.com/news/american-slavery-before-jamestown-1619

3. www.apmresearchlab.org/covid/deaths-by-race

4. www.nytimes.com/2020/06/01/business/economy/black-workers-inequality-economic-risks.html

5. youtu.be/6PXORQE5-CY

6. www.thenation.com/article/archive/hidden-history-alec-and-prison-labor

7. accelresearchsites.com/sugar-rush-how-sugar-consumption-is-changing-america-infographic

8. www.dailymail.co.uk/health/article-3507655/Revealed-body-sugar-weakening-immune-triggering-thrush-terrifying-tool-reveals-exactly-white-stuff-harms-health.html

9. www.diabetes.org/resources/statistics/cost-diabetes

10. www.cdc.gov/nchs/products/databriefs/db360.htm

11. www.apmresearchlab.org/covid/deaths-by-race

12. www.scientificamerican.com/article/how-superspreading-events-drive-most-covid-19-spread1

13. coronavirus.jhu.edu/map.html

14. www.tctmd.com/news/obesitys-role-covid-19-deaths-big-food-slow-government-blame

15. www.thelancet.com/journals/landia/article/PIIS2213-8587(20)30238-2/fulltext

16. clf.jhsph.edu/sites/default/files/2020-02/true-cost-for-food-system-reform-2020.pdf

17. www.cdc.gov/pcd/issues/2019/18_0555.htm

18. sustainableagriculture.net/our-work/campaigns/fbcampaign/what-is-the-farm-bill

19. youtu.be/m0-oC_49fq4

20. www.brookings.edu/research/new-census-data-shows-the-nation-is-diversifying-even-faster-than-predicted

21. en.wikipedia.org/wiki/A_Theory_of_Justice

22. en.wikipedia.org/wiki/World_Happiness_Report

23. www.businessinsider.fr/us/
    what-amazon-ceo-jeff-bezos-makes-every-day-hour-minute-2018-10

24. nccdh.ca/resources/entry/the-spirit-level

25. www.washingtonpost.com/technology/2019/10/29/survey-average-time-
    young-people-spend-watching-videos-mostly-youtube-has-doubled-since

26. www.businessinsider.com/
    dscout-research-people-touch-cell-phones-2617-times-a-day-2016-7

27. guilfordjournals.com/doi/pdf/10.1521/jscp.2018.37.10.751

28. www.npr.org/sections/health-shots/2020/01/23/798676465/
    most-americans-are-lonely-and-our-workplace-culture-may-not-be-helping

29. www.thesocialdilemma.com/

30. youtu.be/kc_Jq42Og7Q

31. www.telegraph.co.uk/technology/2020/05/03/
    meet-ex-google-engineer-built-youtubes-terrifying-recommendations

32. www.newscientist.com/article/2163226-fake-news-travels-six-times-faster-
    than-the-truth-on-twitter/

33. www.theguardian.com/media/2019/feb/18/reporter-jason-rezaian-on-544-
    days-in-iranian-jail-they-never-touched-me-but-i-was-tortured

34. en.wikipedia.org/wiki/Assassination_of_Jamal_Khashoggi

35. www.npr.org/series/5033105/vioxx-the-downfall-of-a-drug

36. www.nytimes.com/2018/05/29/health/purdue-opioids-oxycontin.html

37. www.npr.org/sections/goatsandsoda/2019/05/03/719037789/
    botched-vaccine-launch-has-deadly-repercussions

38. www.nytimes.com/2020/09/02/opinion/coronavirus-vaccine-trump.html

39. www.healthaffairs.org/do/10.1377/hblog20200915.995263/full/

40. www.nih.gov/news-events/news-releases/
    nih-expands-clinical-trials-test-convalescent-plasma-against-covid-19

41. www.politico.com/magazine/story/2019/01/25/
    joe-biden-2019-profile-grief-beau-car-accident-224178

42. www.ekrfoundation.org/